UNDERSTANDING
EARLY YEARS
MATHEMATICS

Derek Haylock lectures in mathematics education at the University of East Anglia, Norwich, where he is the Middle Years (7–12) Course Director. He has considerable experience of initial teacher training, INSET and classroom-based research in mathematics education. He is a regular contributor to mathematics education journals, both in the UK and USA.

Anne Cockburn recently joined the lecturing staff at the University of East Anglia where she is Course Director for the Early Years (4–8). She has extensive experience in classroom-based research and her publications include *The Quality of Pupil Learning Experiences* (S. N. Bennett, C. W. Desforges, A. D. Cockburn and B. Wilkinson), Lawrence Erlbaum Associates, Hillside, NJ. 1984 and *Understanding the Mathematics Teacher: A Study of First School Practice* (with C. W. Desforges, Falmer Press, Lewes, 1987).

UNDERSTANDING EARLY YEARS MATHEMATICS

DEREK HAYLOCK
and ANNE COCKBURN

P·C·P
Paul Chapman
Publishing Ltd

First published 1989

Paul Chapman Publishing Ltd
144 Liverpool Road
London
N1 1LA

British Library Cataloguing in Publication Data
Haylock, Derek W.
  Understanding early years mathematics.
  1. Primary schools. Curriculum subjects. Mathematics
  I. Title   II. Cockburn, Anne
  372.7'3044

ISBN 1-85396-074-8

Typeset by DP Photosetting, Aylesbury, Bucks
Printed in Great Britain by St. Edmundsbury Press,
Bury St Edmunds, Suffolk

CONTENTS

ACKNOWLEDGEMENTS

Many people helped to create this book. In particular we would like to express our appreciation to those teachers who attended our in-service course at the University of East Anglia, Norwich, and who were so willing to discuss openly their own queries and confusions about the mathematics they have to teach in their classrooms: to the two Marys, Enid, Averil, Diana, Cathy, Laura, Lesley, June, Maxine, Suzanne and Amanda, thank you. Our acknowledgements also go to the many teachers, pupils, colleagues and students who over the years have helped us to formulate our ideas. Finally we should thank Christina, Catherine, Jenny and Dusty for their tolerance of the impositions put upon them in the preparation of this book.

INTRODUCTION

Understanding Early Years Mathematics is a book for those who teach or who are preparing to teach mathematics in infant or primary schools and who wish to have a clearer understanding of the mathematical ideas behind the material they deal with in the classroom. For many people mathematics is a subject that generates a feeling of unease and insecurity. Those of us who sometimes have to admit that we are in some sense 'mathematicians' become used to responses such as:

- You must be very clever if you teach maths!
- I never really understood maths at school. I just learnt to do the tricks.
- Oh, no, not maths! I'm hopeless at maths.

What is it about mathematics that makes it seem so difficult? Why does this subject cause so much anxiety and unease? Need we be afraid of it? If you were hopeless at mathematics at school is there any chance that you will ever understand it, or even enjoy it?

This book is not written for those who can solve sixty mathematical problems in sixty seconds while standing on their heads doing the ironing. Rather it is intended for those who feel inadequate when a mathematically-gifted 6-year-old poses an awkward question; for those who have sometimes wondered exactly what are the meanings of mathematical symbols such as the equals sign, but never dared admit it; for those who worry that some of the things they say when they are teaching mathematics to young children might not be absolutely correct.

We do not claim to have all the answers, but we hope that this book might help to remove some of the mysteries. We hope that we can demonstrate that understanding of mathematics need not be the sole prerogative of those who call themselves mathematicians. It is not a book of superficial tips for teachers, and we guarantee that you will not be able to canter through it. We hope that it is a book that will make you pause for thought and reassess your own understanding of basic mathematical ideas. It might even make you a better teacher of mathematics to young children, by increasing your confidence and dispelling some of the fears and anxieties you might have about this area of the curriculum.

Our interest in writing this book arose from our concern over the long-term effects on pupils of their teachers' mathematical misconceptions and limited understanding of the subject. Frequently – through no fault of their own – even the most conscientious and able teachers do not consciously articulate these limitations. This is no doubt simply because they and their teachers before them were taught mathematics by drill, as a set of rules and recipes. Understanding as a goal may have played little part in their mathematics education.

For example, we have found that very few teachers have other than a limited understanding of something as basic as subtraction. The subtraction symbol is invariably associated with the words 'take away', which is but one of at least five different models for this operation. As we discuss in Chapter 3 of this book, other models, such as comparison and inverse of addition, have much more significance in the long term. Unless young children have experience of these models built into their understanding of the subtraction concept, it seems likely that they will face difficulties later when they encounter a statement such as '3 – (–4) = 7'. After all, how can you take something away from 3 and end up with more than you started with? It is our view that teachers of mathematics to young children need to sort out and clarify in their own minds such mathematical ideas.

To explore the nature of infant and primary teachers' mathematical understanding we invited twelve teachers of 5 – 8-year-olds to the University of East Anglia, Norwich, over a six-week period to discuss their own mathematical needs in the light of their experience of teaching the subject to young children. Numerous queries and doubts about mathematical ideas that turn up in school mathematics activities were articulated. Gradually, gaping holes in mathematical knowledge were exposed and plugged, as we talked together about the nature of understanding of such basic mathematical ideas as number, place value, equality, addition, subtraction, multiplication, division, measurement, and space and shape. The satisfaction expressed by the teachers with whom we worked as previously-fuzzy ideas began to fall into place led us confidently to use the material from these discussions as the basis for this book. The first chapter introduces some important themes that ran through all our discussions: the relationships between language, symbols, concrete experience and pictures in mathematical understanding, and the fundamental role of the concepts of transformation and equivalence.

Questions and observations raised by the teachers with whom we worked (and, occasionally, other teachers) are used throughout as illustrative material, as well as examples of children's mathematical thinking. Although the book focuses on the understanding of mathematical ideas rather than on how to teach mathematics, pedagogical implications are considered where appropriate, and each chapter concludes with some suggestions for activities with children, designed to enhance understanding of the ideas discussed in the chapter.

At the time of writing, practitioners in England and Wales are facing up to the demands of implementing the National Curriculum proposals for mathematics, with national assessments at ages 7 and 11. As they do this, they will no doubt recognize the importance of themselves having a thorough understanding of the basic mathematical ideas that will underlie the attainment targets and programmes of study for the early years of schooling. This book aims to develop that understanding.

Derek Haylock and Anne Cockburn
University of East Anglia, Norwich
School of Education

1
MATHEMATICAL SYMBOLS

I thought 6-year-old Gemma had a good understanding of the equals sign. She had no problem with sums like 2 + 3 = □ and 8 + □ = 9. Then I asked her how she did 2 + □ = 6. She replied, 'I said to myself 2, 3, 4, 5, 6 and so the answer is 4. Sometimes I do them the other way round, but it doesn't make any difference.' She pointed to 1 + □ = 10. 'For this one I did 10 and 1 and that's 11.'

This book is about understanding. It has arisen from an attempt to help teachers to understand some of the mathematical ideas children handle in the early years of schooling. It is based on our experience that many teachers and students are helped enormously in their teaching of mathematics by a shift in their perception of the subject away from the learning of a collection of recipes and rules towards the development of understanding of mathematical concepts and principles.

For many children, like Gemma in the example above, doing mathematics appears to be a matter of moving symbols around and writing them on pieces of paper, using an apparently arbitrary collection of rules. Of course, mathematics does involve the manipulation of symbols. But the learning of recipes for answering various types of questions is not the basis of understanding in mathematics. In this chapter we will explore the relationship between mathematical symbols and the other components of children's experience of mathematics, and suggest a framework for discussing understanding in mathematics. As two examples, we will discuss understanding of place-value notation and understanding of the equals sign. But we begin with one teacher's description of an example of some children engaged in a mathematical activity designed to develop what we would recognize as some aspects of understanding of the idea of division.

SYMBOLS, CONCRETE EXPERIENCES, LANGUAGE AND PICTURES

Three children, aged about 7, were exploring the early ideas of division. On their table they had a box of toy cars, paper and pencil, a collection of cards with various words written on them – 'shared, between, is, each, sets, of, makes, altogether, three, six, nine, twelve' – and a calculator.

Their first task was to share six cars between the three of them. They discussed the result. Then they selected various cards to make up sentences (Figure 1.1) to describe what they had discovered. The children drew pictures of their sharing (Figure 1.2) and

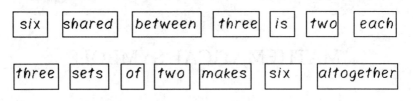

Figure 1.1　Important language patterns for a sharing experience

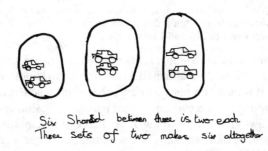

Figure 1.2　Division language linked with a picture ...

copied their two sentences underneath. One of the children then picked up the calculator and interpreted the first sentence by pressing the keys '6 ÷ 3 ='. She seemed delighted to see appear in the display a symbol representing the two cars they each had. She then interpreted their second sentence by pressing '× 2 =' and, as she expected, got back to the six she started with. She demonstrated this to the other children who then insisted on doing it themselves. When they next recorded their calculations as '6 ÷ 3 = 2' and '2 × 3 = 6', the symbols were a record of the keys pressed on the calculator and the resulting display. Later on I will get them to include with their drawings, their sentences and their recording in symbols, a number-line picture like this (see Figure 1.3).

A simple model that enables us to talk about understanding in mathematics is to view the growth of understanding as the building up of (cognitive) connections. More specifically, when we encounter some new experience there is a sense in which we understand it if we can connect it to previous experiences or, better, to a network of previously-connected experiences. The more strongly connected the experience, the more we understand it. Learning without making connections is what we would call learning by rote. The teacher's role in developing understanding is, then, to help the child to build up connections between new experiences and previous learning.

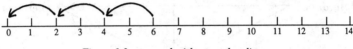

Figure 1.3   ... and with a number line

When children are engaged in mathematical activity, as in the example above, they are involved in manipulating some or all of the following: concrete materials, symbols, language and pictures. They manipulate concrete materials – moving blocks, various sets of objects and toys, rods, counters, fingers, coins, and so forth. They manipulate symbols – making marks on pieces of paper, arranging them in the prescribed fashion, copying exercises from the workcard, numbering the questions, drawing lines here and there, crossing out some symbols, carrying one, filling in boxes, underlining the answer, and so on, or pressing buttons on their calculator. They manipulate language – reading workcards, making sentences incorporating specific mathematical words, processing the teacher's instructions, interpreting word problems, saying out loud the words that go with their recording. And finally, they manipulate pictures – number lines, set diagrams, arrow pictures, graphs, and so on.

We find it very helpful to think of understanding the concepts of number and number operations (i.e. number, addition, subtraction, multiplication, division, equals, and so on) as involving the building up of a network of cognitive connections between these four types of experience: concrete experiences, symbols, language and pictures. Any one of the arrows in Figure 1.4 represents a possible connection between experiences that might form part of the understanding of a mathematical concept.

In the example described above of children engaged in some simple division activities, we have seen them developing understanding in this sense. They are connecting their manipulation of their toy cars with the language patterns of '... shared between ... is ... each', and '... sets of ... makes ... altogether'. They are connecting their concrete experience with a picture of three sets of two things. The language of their sentences is connected with the symbols on the keys and display of the calculator. And then, later, they will be learning to interpret these symbols as a picture of three steps of two on a number line.

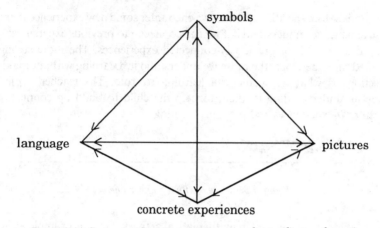

Figure 1.4 Some significant connections in understanding mathematics

PLACE-VALUE NOTATION

The connections framework outlined above is, of course, only a model designed to enable us to discuss and to recognize some aspects of understanding in mathematics. As an example of its use we will consider understanding of the important concept of place value.

This is the basis of our Hindu-Arabic number system that enables us to represent all numbers by using just ten digits. The value that each digit represents is determined by its place (going from right to left), the first place representing ones, the second tens, the next hundreds, and so on, with increasing powers of ten. Thus the digit 9 in 900 represents a value ten times greater than it does in the figure 90. Most teachers would agree that a proper understanding of place value is an essential basis for progress in arithmetic.

What is involved in understanding this concept? What connections between symbols, language, concrete experiences and pictures might be established as part of this understanding? First, the child will experience the principle of exchange in a variety of concrete situations, learning to connect the manipulation of materials with the language pattern 'one of these ... ten of those'. This might be working with base-ten materials, as shown in Figure 1.5, where a flat piece can literally be constructed from ten long pieces, or with 1p, 10p and 100p coins, in which one coin is worth ten of another sort. Children would demonstrate understanding of this principle of exchange when they reduce a collection of base-ten materials, or 1p, 10p, 100p coins, to the smallest number of pieces or coins by a process of exchange, using the appropriate language of exchange to describe what they are doing: 'one of these is ten of those', or 'one of these is worth ten of those'.

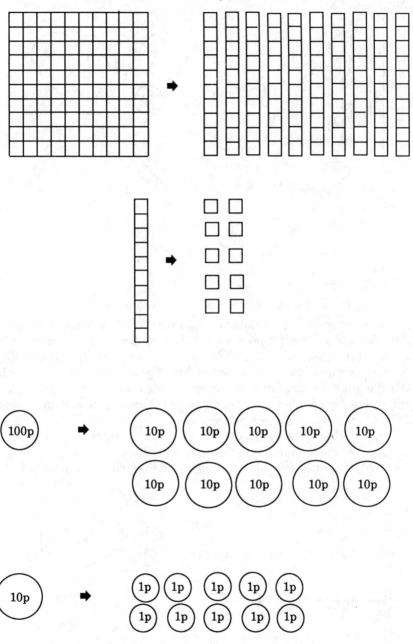

Figure 1.5 'One of these is ten of those'

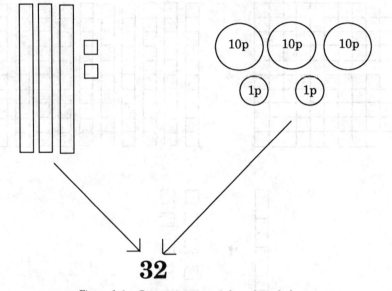

32

Figure 1.6　Connecting materials and symbols

They will learn to connect collections of materials with the symbols, as shown in Figure 1.6. They might demonstrate understanding of this connection by selecting (1) appropriate base-ten blocks or (2) appropriate 1p, 10p and 100p coins, to correspond to any given two- or three-digit number written in symbols. One important component of this understanding is the use of zero as a place holder. For example, in Figure 1.7, the child will learn to connect the symbols 206 with the collection of materials shown.

Understanding place-value notation also involves learning to connect the language of number with the symbols. So, for example, '342' written down or appearing on a calculator display, is connected with 'three hundred and forty-

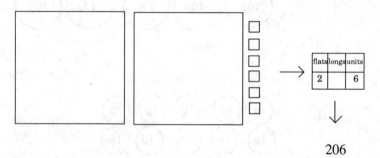

flats	longs	units
2		6

206

Figure 1.7　Zero as a place holder

two', spoken. Again there are particular problems in making these connections where zero occurs. It is also unfortunate that, in common with other European languages, English does not settle down to a systematic relationship between the language and the symbols until we get beyond the number 19. We would find it much easier to help children to connect the language and the symbols if we counted '... seven, eight, nine, ten, onety-one, onety-two, onety-three ...'. We know some teachers who actually do this with children in the early stages of place-value work, as a bridge between numbers up to and numbers beyond 20.

A further aspect of understanding of place value is shown in Figure 1.8. The child learns to connect the symbols with the important picture of the number line. This might involve, for example, locating the approximate position of a given number on a number line labelled (1) in 10s, (2) in 100s or, vice versa, stating or writing the approximate number corresponding to a given point on a number line labelled (1) in 10s, (2) in 100s.

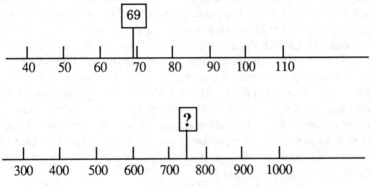

Figure 1.8   Connecting symbols with the number-line picture

We see therefore that much of what is involved in understanding place value can be identified as the building up of a network of connections between language, symbols, concrete materials and pictures. We find it helpful to regard many mathematical concepts as networks of such connections.

WHAT ARE MATHEMATICAL SYMBOLS?

What exactly are mathematical symbols, other than marks we write on paper and learn to manipulate according to various rules? What is the function of a symbol in mathematics? What is the relationship of a mathematical symbol to our experiences of doing mathematics and handling mathematical ideas?

- I think of mathematical symbols as abbreviations. They're a sort of shorthand.

- They have very ambiguous meanings for me. They have different meanings depending on the situation you're using them in.
- They sometimes mean you have to do something. Perform an operation. Move some blocks around.

There is a sense in which mathematical symbols (such as 4, 28, ÷, =) are abbreviations for mathematical ideas or concepts. But it is important to note at the outset that this does not mean that a symbol in mathematics is just an abbreviation for a specific word or phrase. It is tempting to think of, say, the division sign as being essentially an abbreviation for the words 'shared between'. Children appear often to view mathematical symbols in this way. One 9-year-old was using a calculator to do 28 ÷ 4, saying to himself as he pressed the buttons, 'Twenty-eight shared ...'. At this point he turned to the teacher and asked, 'Which button's between?' It was as though each word had to have a button or a symbol to represent it. When we see children writing 41 for fourteen it is clear that they often say 'four' and write 4, then say 'teen' and write 1, again using the symbols as abbreviations for the sounds they are uttering. And so the same child will happily write 41 for forty-one a few lines later! We see a similar error when children record a number like three hundred and seventy-five as 30075 or 3075. The noughts are written down as abbreviations for the word 'hundred'.

But once we begin to think of understanding, particularly understanding of number and number operations, as the building up of connections between concrete experiences, symbols, words and pictures, we begin to see that a mathematical symbol is not an abbreviation for just one category of concrete experiences, or just one word or phrase, or just one picture. The child has to learn to connect one symbol with a potentially-confusing variety of concrete situations, pictures and language.

Hence we would suggest that a symbol in mathematics is a way of representing a concept, a network of connections. The symbol then becomes a means whereby we can manipulate that concept according to precise rules. Without the symbols it would be virtually impossible for us to manipulate the concepts. The symbols of mathematics allow us both to discover and to express relationships between various concepts. For example, when we write down a statement like '2 + 4 = 6' we are expressing a relationship between the numbers two, four and six, the operation of addition and the notion of equality.

The teacher's suggestion above that mathematical symbols have different meanings depending on the situation in which they are being used is a very perceptive observation. One symbol might indeed represent a complex network of connections, and can therefore be applied to a variety of situations and pictures, and associated with a variety of language. This is at one and the same time the reason why mathematics is so powerful, and probably the reason why – for many – it is such a difficult subject to understand.

THE EQUALS SIGN

Consider, for example, the equals sign: '='. We shall see that it is precisely because a concept like 'equals' is such a complex network of ideas and experiences that we find there is not just one form of words that goes with the symbol '=' and there is a whole range of situations to which the symbol becomes attached. Some of their anxieties about the meaning of this symbol were articulated by some of the infant teachers with whom we worked:

- My 6-year-olds had problems with some questions in their maths books where they had to put in the missing numbers, like this: $6 = 2 + \square$. Most of them put in 8, of course. When I tried to explain to them how to do these sums I realized I didn't actually know what the equals sign meant myself. We would say '2 add something makes 6' if it were written the other way round, but '6 makes 2 add something' doesn't make sense.
- Is it wrong to say '4 add 2 makes 6'? Should I insist that the children say 'equals 6'?
- The word 'equals' doesn't mean anything to them. It's just a symbol, just some marks on paper that you make when you're doing sums.
- Doesn't it confuse children to say 'makes' when you're adding and then to say 'leaves' when you're taking away?
- And sometimes we just read it as 'is', like '3 add 4 is 7'.

To analyse the concept associated with the equals sign, we will first discuss two fundamental concepts that run right through mathematics. These are the concepts of *transformation* and *equivalence*.

Figure 1.9 represents two pieces of paper, one A4 size and the other A5 size. Perhaps we should explain that you obtain A1 paper by folding A0 paper in half, A2 by folding A1, and so on, and that the dimensions of the paper are cunningly

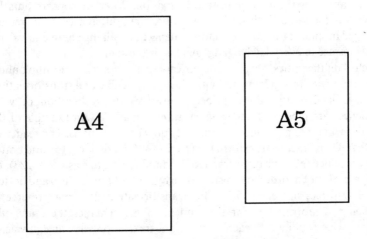

Figure 1.9   The same but different

chosen so that each rectangle has exactly the same proportions as the original. (If you want to be really technical, the sides of the rectangle are in the ratio 1 to the square root of 2, i.e. 1 to 1.414 approximately. And to add to the fun, A0 paper has an area of 1 m².) The upshot of all this is that the A5 rectangle is the shape produced by folding in half the A4 rectangle. Now when we begin to make mathematical statements about the relationships between the two rectangles in Figure 1.9, we find they fall into two categories.

On the one hand, we may look at the rectangles and make observations about the ways in which they differ: one is on the left and the other is on the right, one is half the area of the other, the length of one is 1.414 times the length of the other, and so on. Statements like these are essentially using the concept of transformation. We are concerned with the changes that occur when we move our attention from one rectangle to the other. We are hinting at what would have to be done to one rectangle to transform it to the other.

On the other hand, we may look at these rectangles and make statements about the ways in which they are the same: they are both rectangles, they are the same shape, their sides are in the same proportion. Statements like these are essentially using the concept of equivalence. We are concerned with what stays the same when we move our attention from one rectangle to the other. We are hinting at the existence of a set of shapes, called an *equivalence class*, of which these two are members. All the members of an equivalence class of shapes have some particular property or properties in common that would in certain circumstances allow us to refer to them as the same shape.

More generally, when we make statements about what has changed in a situation, what is different about two things, what something has become, and so on, we are using the concept of transformation. When we concern ourselves with what is the same, with similarities rather than differences, what remains unchanged in spite of the transformation, then we are talking about equivalence. The key phrase in everyday language here is 'is the same as'.

Much of mathematics, not just geometrical experiences like the example above, is concerned with recognizing and applying equivalences and transformations. Often a crucial mathematical principle involves the recognition of which equivalences are preserved under which transformations. An example of this, which illustrates the point nicely, is that of equivalent fractions. The reader will recall that it's in order to transform the fraction 4/6, by dividing top and bottom by 2, to produce the equivalent fraction 2/3 (and record this as 4/6 = 2/3). But it is apparently not in order to transform 4/6 by, say, adding 1 to top and bottom, because 4/6 does not equal 5/7. This transformation does not preserve the equivalence. Unfortunately for the student of mathematics there are other situations where adding 1 to each of two numbers does preserve an equivalence, such as when calculating the difference between two numbers (e.g. 77 – 49 can be correctly and usefully transformed into 78 – 50). At times one feels sorry for the poor pupils trying to make sense of this subject – it must seem to be quite arbitrary as to whether a particular transformation is acceptable and warrants a red tick or is unacceptable and generates a red cross.

Strictly speaking, then, the equals sign represents this concept of equivalence. When we write down '2 + 4 = 6' we are expressing an equivalence between '2 + 4' and '6'. We are making a statement that there is something the same about 'two added to four' and 'six'. Probably the most straightforward language to go with this statement is 'two add four is the same as six'. To emphasize the underlying equivalence in arithmetic statements using the equals sign, the phrase 'is the same as' is particularly significant. It connects very clearly with the concrete experience of doing addition and subtraction with materials such as Stern blocks, or Cuisenaire or colour-factor rods (see Figure 1.10). When the child makes a train with a 2-rod and a 4-rod the problem is to find another rod to match this train. Recording the experience as '2 + 4 = 6' is an expression of the equivalence: the 2-rod added to the 4-rod is in one sense the same as the 6-rod. Of course, they are only the same in that they are the same length. A train made up of a blue rod and a brown rod is very different from a red rod. But lying there side by side they represent an equivalence, and this is expressed by the symbols '2 + 4 = 6'. It is worth noting that this interpretation of the equals sign makes sense of the problem we started with: '6 = 2 + □' is read as 'six is the same as two add something'.

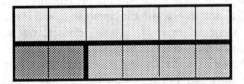

Figure 1.10 '*Two add four is the same as six*'

However, when the child puts out sets of two counters and four counters, forms their union and counts the new set to discover that there is now a set of six counters, it is a bit obscure to suggest that this is an experience of 'two add four is the same as six'. The child has transformed the two sets of two and four counters into a set of six (Figure 1.11). The child's attention, therefore, is focused on the transformation that has taken place. This being so, it seems perfectly natural and surely appropriate to use the language 'two and four makes six' to describe the transformation the child has effected. One teacher said that she regarded the symbols as instructions to do something – in other words, to apply some sort of transformation. There is plenty of evidence that this is how children interpret the equals sign.

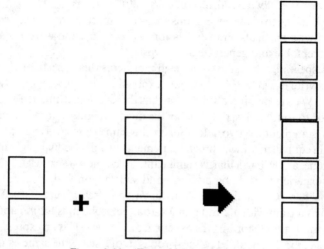

Figure 1.11 '*Two add four makes six*'

It is presumably to emphasize this transformation aspect that some mathematics schemes use an arrow rather than an equals sign to record activities of this sort, for example, writing '2 + 4 → 6'. However, we are taking the view that in practice the equals sign represents both the equivalence and the transformation aspects of the relationship betweeen '2 + 4' and '6'. Thus, we would not want to suggest that it is wrong or in some way mathematically incorrect to associate 'makes', 'leaves', 'is', and so on, with the equals sign, and insist on the one form of words 'is the same as' or even 'equals'. Rather, we would advocate a combination of experiences emphasizing both the notions of equivalence and transformation. As we have already argued, mathematical symbols are not just abbreviations for particular words or phrases. We have to recognize that the statement '2 + 4 = 6' is actually at one and the same time a representation in symbols of the transformation that has been applied to two and four, and the equivalence that has emerged between 2 + 4 and 6.

It could be, therefore, that the child's attention might on some occasions be directed to the transformation of two and four into six, particularly when using counters, fingers, sets of toys, pencils, sweets, and so on. And on other occasions, particularly when using some structural apparatus or when making steps on a number line, the attention might be directed to the equivalence of two added to four and six. On both occasions the child might record their activity as '2 + 4 = 6'. But this might be accompanied in the first case by the words 'two add four makes six', and possibly in the second case by the words 'two add four is the same as six'. The use of different language appropriate to the situation is inevitable and perfectly acceptable, demonstrating that the child is gaining experience of both the transformation and the equivalence built into the relationship between '2 + 4' and '6'.

These two ideas of transformation and equivalence are almost always present whenever we make statements of equality. In the fractions example above, when we write down '4/6 = 2/3' we are both recording a transformation that has been applied to the 4/6 and recognizing an equivalence that emerged. There is a sense in which 4/6 is not the same as 2/3. Using one meaning of the fraction notation, four slices of a cake cut into six equal parts is different from two slices of a cake cut into three equal parts. But there is something very significantly the same about these two situations – they produce the same amount of cake – which prompts us to recognize an equivalence and to record it with the equals sign. This is just the same with '2 + 4 = 6'. Two piles of cubes, one containing two and the other containing four, look quite different from a pile of six cubes, yet there is a sameness about the two situations that warrants the use of the equals sign.

So, what does the equals sign mean? Strictly we should concede that it means 'is equivalent to' or 'is the same as', in whatever sense is determined by the context. And we should say that perhaps this is an aspect of the meaning of the symbol that is underplayed by teachers. It would be no bad thing for the children's mathematical development for the phrase 'is the same as' to occur more frequently in their talk and in the talk of their teachers. But as with all mathematical symbols we have to learn to connect the equals sign with a complex variety of situations, operations and language, sometimes focusing on the transformation and sometimes on the equivalence. Understanding mathematics right from the earliest years involves us in learning to attach the same symbol to a potentially-bewildering variety of situations and language. This is even true of the first mathematical symbols we encounter, those used to represent numbers. This is the subject of the next chapter.

SUMMARY OF KEY IDEAS IN CHAPTER 1

1. A simple model for talking about understanding is that to understand something is to connect it with previous learning or other experiences.
2. Mathematical activity involves the manipulation of concrete materials, symbols, language and pictures.
3. Connections between these four types of experience constitute important components of mathematical understanding.
4. A mathematical concept can be thought of as a network of connections between symbols, language, concrete experiences and pictures.
5. A mathematical symbol is a way of representing a mathematical concept that enables us to manipulate it and to discover and express relationships with other concepts.

6. Understanding the concept of place value includes being able to move between the language and symbols used for numbers, concrete experiences with base-ten materials and coins, and the number-line picture.
7. The concepts of equivalence and transformation refer respectively to statements of similarity and statements of difference or change.
8. The equals sign strictly means 'is the same as' or 'is equivalent to'. However, in practice it often represents both an instruction to apply a transformation – in which case language such as 'makes' and 'leaves' is appropriate – and the equivalence that emerges.

SOME ACTIVITIES WITH CHILDREN

At the end of each chapter we have provided some examples of activities teachers might use with children to develop the mathematical ideas explored in the text. The activities are all aimed at developing what we might recognize as understanding, and we hope that they may provide teachers with some indication of ways in which the ideas we have outlined in each chapter might influence their practice. We have deliberately not specified ages for the children. Many of these activities can be used with a wide age-range, either as they are given here or by appropriate modification.

Activity 1.1: connections (add and subtract)

Objective To develop connections between symbols, concrete experiences, language and pictures, using the concepts of addition and subtraction.

Materials A box of counters (or toys or pennies); paper and pencil; strips of card with words written on them – 'take away, add, leaves, makes' – and cards with numbers from 1 to 20 written on them; a calculator; a duplicated sheet of number lines marked from 0 to 20.

Method Develop an activity, for a small group of children, using subtraction and addition, similar to that using division and multiplication outlined at the beginning of this chapter. The children should start with two of the numbered cards, e.g. 12 and 5. They put out twelve counters, move five to one side, count how many are left. They then use the cards to make up two sentences: 'Twelve take away five leaves seven' and 'seven add five makes twelve'. They draw a picture on their paper to show what they have done and write the sentences underneath, as shown in Figure 1.12. They then press the keys on the calculator, which correspond to their actions with the counters: '12 – 5 = 7' and '7 + 5 = 12'. Finally, they must represent the relationship on a number line, as shown in Figure 1.13. Discuss with the children how their number-line diagram shows both '12 – 5' and '7 + 5'.

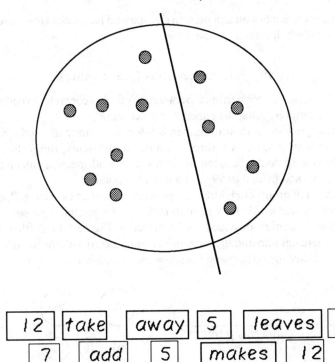

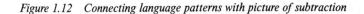

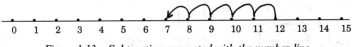

Figure 1.12   Connecting language patterns with picture of subtraction

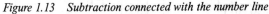

Figure 1.13   Subtraction connected with the number line

Activity 1.2: bundling in tens

Objective To provide topic-based, practical experience of the place-value principle of bundling into tens.

Materials A Paddington Bear; pretend (or real?) biscuits; packing material; and a three-minute timer with a buzzer.

Method This could be an activity for three children, as part of an on-going project on the Paddington Bear theme. Two children package biscuits into rolls of ten at a time, while the third sets the timer going. When the buzzer sounds the third player announces that Paddington has come for his biscuits. This child, with the assistance of Paddington, counts how many biscuits each player has wrapped and awards a biscuit as a prize to the one who has packed the most. The children can take it in turns to be packers.

Activity 1.3: connections (place value)

Objective To develop connections between symbols, concrete experiences, language and pictures, using the concept of place value.

Materials A pack of cards with numerals 0-9 written on them, and strips of card with the words: 'one, two, three, ... nine', and 'twenty, thirty, forty, ... ninety'; 10p and 1p coins; base-ten materials units and longs; a calculator; a number line marked from 0 to 99; and a movable pointer.

Method A small group of children are given two number cards, e.g. 2 and 3, arranged side by side as 23. They have to make all the possible representations of this with the materials provided, as illustrated in Figure 1.14. (Either avoid using 1 in the tens column initially, or consider using a card with the word 'onety' written on it. Later include separate cards with the number names from ten to nineteen.)

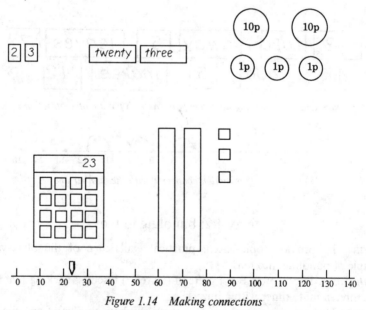

Figure 1.14   Making connections

Activity 1.4: say, press, write

Objective To practise adding or subtracting 1, 10, 100, as part of the understanding of place value.

Materials Pencil and paper; and a calculator with a constant addition facility (most have this).

Method Children work in pairs. The teacher writes on the top of their sheet of paper one of the following instructions: 'Add 1, add 10, add 100, subtract 1, subtract 10, subtract 100', and then underneath this a line of five starting numbers. For example, with 'add 10' the children might have the starting numbers 23, 49, 30, 16 and 4.

For each starting number the children have to produce a column of numbers by continually adding 10 (or whatever the instruction is), e.g. 23, 33, 43, and so on, until they reach the bottom of the page. This is done by a process of 'say, press, write'. The starting number is entered on the calculator, followed by the instruction (e.g. 23 + 10). One child *says* what the next number will be, the other then *presses* the equals key, then, after checking, the first *writes* the result. They then swap over, one *says* the next number, the other *presses* the equals key, and the first *writes* the result. And so on. (If the calculator has a constant-addition facility, all that is required after entering 23 + 10 is continually to press the equals key to obtain each number in the sequence.)

The same process applies with any instruction (+1, +10, +100, –1, –10, –100) and any starting numbers. Teachers should not be frightened to let children investigate subtraction examples where their calculator takes them into negative answers!

Activity 1.5: missing numbers

Objective To help children understand missing number sums and the meaning of the equals sign.

Materials A few Stern blocks or equivalent materials.

Method First investigate how your children handle a collection of missing number sums, where the box for the missing number might be in any one of six positions. For example, using the sum $3 + 5 = 8$:

$$3 + 5 = \square$$
$$3 + \square = 8$$
$$\square + 5 = 8$$
$$\square = 3 + 5$$
$$8 = \square + 5$$
$$8 = 3 + \square$$

Which type of questions do they find easiest? Most difficult? Talk with the children about how they interpret the questions and discover what language they use for the equals sign.

Explore the suggestions that (1) using the phrase 'is the same as' to go with the equals sign, and (2) connecting the symbols in these questions with corresponding manipulations of Stern blocks, might help children to make more sense of them.

SUGGESTIONS FOR FURTHER READING

At the end of each chapter we have included a short list of references that might be of interest to readers wishing to consider specific aspects in more detail. In addition, at the end of the book, we have compiled a brief bibliography of texts we have found particularly useful and informative.

Ashlock, R.B. (1987) 'Use of informal language when introducing concepts', *Focus on Learning Problems in Mathematics*, Vol. 9, no. 3, pp. 31–6. (Ashlock discusses how to avoid some of the confusions that can arise when young children are introduced to formal symbolism and mathematical language.)

Behr, M., Erlwanger, S. and Nichols, E. (1980) 'How children view the equals sign', *Mathematics Teaching*, Vol. 92, pp. 13–15. (This is an account of some interesting research into how 6–7-year-olds respond to number statements of the form '$a + b = \square$' and '$\square = a + b$'. The authors conclude that the equals sign is viewed by children as a 'do something signal', that is, as an operator rather than a means of expressing a relation.)

Dickson, L., Brown, M. and Gibson, O. (1984) *Children Learning Mathematics*, Cassell Education for the Schools Council, London. (Dickson and her colleagues discuss in a detailed and informative manner (pp. 200–21) the meaning of place value and how to teach it.)

Haylock, D. (1982) 'Understanding in mathematics: making connections', *Mathematics Teaching*, Vol. 92, pp. 54–6. (This article outlines the connections model of understanding introduced in this chapter and gives examples of its use in school mathematics.)

Hiebert, J. (1988) 'A theory of developing competence with written mathematical symbols', *Educational Studies in Mathematics*, Vol. 19, pp. 333–55. (Hiebert presents a theory of how competence with written mathematical symbols develops and how the sequencing and the content of instructional activities may be used to reduce the possibility of pupils' mathematical behaviour becoming overly mechanical and inflexible.)

Hughes, M. (1986) *Children and Number*, Blackwell, Oxford. (In Chapter 7 – 'Understanding the written symbolism of arithmetic' – of his book, Hughes describes some of the difficulties children experience when they first encounter written symbolism in mathematics.)

Jones, K. and Haylock, D.W. (1985) 'Developing children's understanding in mathematics', *Remedial Education*, Vol. 20, pp. 30–4. (This article describes how the theoretical framework discussed in this chapter has been translated by teachers into a practical activity with perceptibly encouraging results for mathematically low-attaining children.)

Kamii, C. (1985) *Young Children Reinvent Arithmetic*, Teachers' College Press, New York, NY. (Basing her argument on extensive research and experience, Kamii explains the complexities of place value and reasons that it is an inappropriate topic for infant mathematics.)

Liebeck, P. (1985) 'Reading mathematics', *Mathematics Teaching*, Vol. 110, pp. 14–15. (Liebeck considers popular infant-mathematics schemes and the language they use when first introducing children to symbolic representation.)

2
NUMBER

A 7-year-old child was asked to write a story to go with the symbols '5 – 3':

> Once upon a time there lived a nubere and he was called 5 and he was very lonly. Won day he saw a nubere 3 and he was lonly to saw he went up to him and sad well you be my frinde. Yes he sad becase I have no frinde to play with. Saw five and three were good frinds and they were happy and the nexed day they went four a pikenick and had a good time. They had cakes and drink and sandwich and biskites and they came home and got into bed with a hot water botel.

WHAT IS THREE?

This child's delightfully amusing interpretation of numbers as characters in a story with lives of their own might cause us to pause and ask ourselves what numbers mean to us. What, for example, is three? Close your eyes and bring to the forefront of your mind an image of the number three. Describe the image in your mind.

- I can see three dots arranged in a triangle.
- A set of three fruits, an apple, an orange and a banana.
- Three dots in a line.
- A triangle, a shape with three sides.
- The symbol 3.
- Someone holding up three fingers.

This question has been asked to hundreds of teachers and student teachers and almost invariably the responses are similar to those above, falling into two categories: either the image described is a set of three things, dots, sides of a triangle, fingers, sweets, vague unspecified objects or splodges, and so on; or, less frequently, the picture imagined is just the symbol 3.

Clearly the symbol is not the number. As discussed in Chapter 1, the symbol allows us to represent the concept of three and to manipulate it and to relate it to other numbers. But the actual symbol we use is fairly arbitrary. Other cultures use other symbols and other words, but the same concept of three lies behind them. If occasionally we want to distinguish the symbol from the number it represents, then we can refer to the *numeral* 3. Numerals are the marks we make on paper, such as 3, 26, 819, when we record and manipulate numbers. Incidentally, in our discussion of place value in Chapter 1 we have already used the word *digits* to refer to the 8, the 1 and the 9 in the numeral 819.

The image of three that clearly dominates the thinking of most adults, and presumably that of the children we teach, is the idea that three is a set of three things. When the infant teacher needs to explain a problem involving the number 3 to a child, the most likely thing to appear on the desk will be a set of three counters, three blocks, or if nothing else comes readily to hand, three fingers. It could be suggested then that 'three' is actually what all these sets of three things have in common. Three is seen as a concept abstracted from many examples of sets of three things. One-to-one matching of objects in one set of three with objects in another set of three, as illustrated in Figure 2.1, is designed to concentrate the child's perception on what is the same about the two sets.

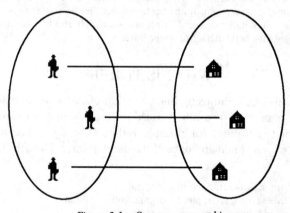

Figure 2.1   One-to-one matching

Again we see the notions of transformation and equivalence in operation. For example, when a child matches a set of three cups, one to one, on to a set of three saucers, the operation of matching shifts the focus away from the differences between the cups and the saucers in favour of what is the same about them, namely their threeness.

Here's an interesting question: is three an adjective or a noun?

• It must be an adjective, because you talk about three things. Three apples, three

bananas and so on. It describes the set.
- I think it can be both.
- To convince me that it can be a noun you need to give me a sentence beginning with the words 'three is ...'.
- Three is a number.
- Three is less than five.
- Three is a factor of twelve.
- Three is a prime number.

When three changes from an adjective to a noun like this it is no longer attached to the sets of three things, it has a life of its own. We can talk about 'three' as though it exists independently of the sets to which we might connect it. It could be suggested that a key stage in the development of the concept of number is this transition from number as an adjective to number as a noun.

CARDINAL AND ORDINAL

In fact, this view of the way in which number concepts develop is very simplistic and makes little allowance for the complex network of connections between concrete experience, language, pictures and the symbol 3, which constitute the concept of three. So far we have only talked about connecting the symbol with concrete situations consisting of sets of three things. This is only one aspect of a number, referred to as the *cardinal* aspect. But to what else, apart from sets of things, can we attach the symbol 3?

- What about the 3 on a clock face – that's not denoting a set of three things, is it?
- I live at number 3, but I don't live in a set of three houses!
- Or page 3 in a newspaper?
- It's like the number 3 bus. It's just a label that helps us identify one bus from another.

The 3 on a number 3 bus is indeed just a label, a number used, in what is called the *nominal* aspect, just to label items and to distinguish them from one another. Behind the other responses is another very important category of images of the number 3. This is called the *ordinal* aspect of number: numbers used to label things but also to put them in order. Room number 3, house number 3, the 3 on the clock face, page 3 in a book – these are labelled 3 because in some ordering system they come between 2 and 4. Notice that there is no 'threeness' in the cardinal sense about this use of the number 3. Page 3 is not a set of three pages, it doesn't necessarily contain a photograph of three people or three objects, nor does it contain just three words or three sentences. It's labelled 3 simply because it is located between page 2 and page 4.

We want to emphasize that this is not an obscure or secondary aspect of the concept of number in spite of the fact that almost none of us brings to mind an ordinal image when asked to think of three. This ordinal aspect of the number is as central and important as the cardinal aspect, and one we use all the time in our everyday lives whether it be finding our page in a book, locating a room in a strange building, looking up a date on a calendar or deciding whether it's our turn to pad up ready for the next wicket to fall.

COUNTING

It is, of course, in counting that the cardinal and ordinal aspects come together. What is involved in counting? First of all the child learns a pattern of noises, memorized by repetition in all sorts of situations both in and out of school: 'One, two, three, . . . and so on'. This set of sounds is probably just as meaningless as many traditional nursery rhymes, serving merely to demonstrate the young child's amazing capacity for sequential learning. Then the child has to learn to co-ordinate the utterance of these noises with the physical movements of a finger and the eye along a line of objects, matching one noise to one object. The two-syllable word 'seven' sometimes poses a particularly difficult problem of co-ordination! As each number is spoken it is being used in an ordinal sense, to label the objects and to order them – number one, number two, and so on. But then the child has somehow to discover that the ordinal number of the last object is the cardinal number of the set. What a stunning and powerful discovery this is! One 4-year-old was counting objects in her head and suddenly announced with great excitement, 'Three is three, isn't it!' More counting, then, 'Four is four! And five is five!' It was as though she was counting to three and then realizing that when you got to three you actually had a set of three things, and similarly with four and five.

A NETWORK OF CONNECTIONS

The importance of the ordinal aspect means, therefore, that a very significant part of understanding number is the connection between the symbols and the picture of number incorporated in a number line, one example of which is shown in Figure 2.2. Possibly even more effective for developing number concepts is a similar line arranged vertically, so that the numbers become larger as you go up and smaller as you go down. Either of these lines is a picture of number that

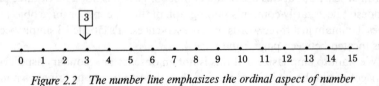

Figure 2.2   The number line emphasizes the ordinal aspect of number

particularly emphasizes the ordinal aspect. Another example incorporating this ordinal aspect would be a number strip – a line of squares numbered in order – as occurs in many board games. The number three is one point on the number line, or one square on the number strip, not three points or three squares, and its main property is that it lies between two and four.

It appears, therefore, that the answer to the question, 'What is three?' is far from straightforward. The concept of a number like three appears to involve a network of connections between the symbol 3, the word 'three', concrete situations of sets of things using the cardinal aspect and pictures of number involving the ordinal aspect, such as number lines. Hence it seems that at a very early age the child encounters one enormous difficulty that runs right through mathematics: that one symbol is used to represent vastly different situations. Not just different in the way in which a set of three sweets is different from a set of three plates, but as different as the questions, 'How many pages have you read today?' and 'What page are you on?' Both questions might elicit a response of 'three', but with two completely different meanings.

Of course, the different meanings of the symbol are not totally unrelated and arbitrary as, for example, two different meanings of some words might be, such as 'well' (in good health) and 'well' (of water). But the connections are by no means at a simple level of perception and the teacher has a major task to help the child to make the connections and to build them into a coherent network. Nor are the cardinal and ordinal aspects of number the whole story. Consider the use of number in the following sentence, overheard when a teacher was talking to a group of children: 'There are three children in class four who are five.' This demonstrates the way in which we expect even young children to connect number symbols and words to very different situations. In the space of ten simple words the teacher has used numbers in three widely-differing ways. The three children constitute a cardinal 3 and class four is an ordinal 4. The five (years old) is an example of number used in a measuring context. The different ways in which numbers are used in measurement are discussed in Chapter 5.

It is important for teachers of young children to lay foundations of experience and networks of connections on to which future experiences of number can be built. In this respect the cardinal aspect of number is a very limited view of what numbers are. It is not difficult, for example, to extend your understanding of numbers to make connections with negative numbers if the ordinal aspect and the associated picture of the number line is a strong part of your concept of number. All that is required is to extend the number line the other side of zero and to use appropriate labels for the new points. In a local department store the buttons in the lift are labelled 3, 2, 1 and 0 for the third, second, first and ground floors. How mathematically pleasing to note that the button for the basement is labelled –1! This is a straightforward and obvious extension of ordinal number.

We would argue, therefore, that young children should do as much of their number work moving up and down number lines, or similar manifestations of the ordinal aspect, as they do manipulating sets of counters and blocks, so that they connect the symbol 3 and the word 'three' just as much with the idea of a label for a point or a position as with sets of things. We cannot stress too strongly that *numbers are not just about sets of things*.

We have talked about mathematical concepts as networks of connections between concrete situations, symbols, language and pictures, and highlighted the problem that understanding the concept involves one symbol being connected to a wide range of often very different situations. We have seen that even the basic and seemingly elementary concept of number has this problem built into it, with the same numeral being applied to very different experiences. The discussion about the possible over-emphasis on the cardinal aspect at the expense of the ordinal aspect raises another point of general applicability and great significance to infant teachers. There is a danger that we might continually reinforce just one particular connection in the network of connections constituting a mathematical concept at the expense of equally-important or even ultimately more-significant connections. If this one connection dominates the child's thinking about the concept, then it may be difficult later on to build on new experiences that do not readily connect with this part of the network. For example, if the idea that numbers are sets of things is continually reinforced in the early years and is the dominant connection, then it is not surprising that negative numbers appear very mysterious when they are met later on. You can't think of –3 as a set of things! And if you cannot make connections with previous learning then no understanding but only rote learning can occur.

Learning with understanding progresses most smoothly by what Piaget calls a process of assimilation of new ideas into existing networks of connections. When material does not connect readily to the existing network, then understanding can only be achieved by a restructuring of that network in order to accommodate the new experiences. Many pupils clearly fail to achieve these restructurings, particularly in mathematics, and continue with their limited and inadequate networks of connections. It is because of this that we are emphasizing the importance of infant teachers providing experiences of number early on, particularly activities with the number line, which will provide a basis for later learning with understanding when pupils encounter numbers other than those used for counting.

ZERO

Close your eyes and think of zero. Describe the image in your mind:

- It's very hard to think of nothing!

- I can see a set with nothing in it, like a circle with nothing inside.
- I thought of putting out three chocolates then eating them!

Is zero a number? Many people feel that it isn't really a proper number, not like one, two or three. It's just nothing. In fact it's not uncommon for the word 'nothing' to be attached quite freely to the symbol 0.

A group of student teachers were given a table showing the numbers of children in a class with birthdays in each month, and they were asked which month had the smallest number of birthdays. Some of them had great difficulty in accepting that the month without any birthdays had the smallest number! This fixation with the idea that zero is nothing is, of course, part of the over-emphasis on the cardinal aspect of number. If you have a set of 0 objects in your hand then, of course, you have nothing in your hand. But we have already seen that the cardinal view of a number is very limited. Once we consider the ordinal aspect, zero is then not just as good a number as any other but becomes a very significant and important number. It is the point before one on the number line, and sometimes the starting point; it is the ground floor in the department store; it is midnight on a digital watch – and a temperature of zero degrees is certainly not an absence of temperature!

So understanding the concept of zero involves connecting the symbol and the language, not just with 'nothing' and empty sets but also with ordinal pictures of number where zero is very definitely something:

- The problem is that we sometimes call it zero, we sometimes call it nought and sometimes nothing. Other numbers like one have only one name.
- When children do take-away sums and get nothing left they tend to say 'nothing', but when they count backwards they always say 'zero' at the end, like a countdown for a spaceship.
- Counting backwards is very clearly an ordinal aspect of number, isn't it?
- Do books have a page number zero?

Does this one? How could you label the pages that come before page 1?

A NOTE ON NEGATIVE NUMBERS

We would like to suggest at this point that if greater emphasis is given to the ordinal aspect then negative numbers become very much easier to understand than fractions and decimals. There is, therefore, a good case for introducing them to children before any formal work on fractions or decimals, using appropriate contexts such as number lines, temperatures, page numbers in a book and lifts. One teacher reported her experience of using a number line with 5-year-olds:

I put a vertical number line on the wall with zero and numbers written above it, up to about 10. We did some counting forwards and backwards. Start at 3 and count forward two. Where do you get to? That sort of thing. I had marked some points below zero, but not labelled them. I then asked them to start at 1 and count back three. They did this quite happily and one of the girls amazed me by saying that the point we had arrived at was minus two! I don't know where she got this idea from, but the others picked it up immediately and handled the idea with no difficulty. One of the children pointed out that there was the same pattern of numbers above zero as below zero.

Other teachers have found that young children can link this kind of number-line experience of negative numbers with their experience of repeatedly subtracting 1 on a calculator and slipping quite naturally and confidently below zero in the answers displayed.

A MATHEMATICAL ANALYSIS OF NUMBER

In this section we outline the development of number from a mathematical point of view. Although this introduces some fairly abstract mathematical material, the infant teachers we have worked with were unanimous that the analysis was both comprehensible and helpful to them in their own understanding of what they are doing in teaching number to young children. It is also important for those laying the foundations of number to know what later ideas will have to be built on to those foundations, so that they do not limit children's experiences of number to those which are only appropriate to the numbers we use for counting.

Moving outwards from the centre of Figure 2.3, we will see that this development of number begins with the positive whole numbers, the numbers we use for counting, called the *natural numbers*, then proceeds to expand the set of numbers to what are called *integers*, then *rational numbers*, and finally *real numbers*. Notice that each of these sets includes the previous sets. In the course of the following analysis we will consider each set of numbers in turn. Although the material here is directed at developing the teacher's own understanding of what numbers are, at each stage some pedagogical implications will become apparent. One important theme is that as we move from one set to the next larger set certain mathematical properties change. In fact some things that are true become no longer true, some things that are false become true and some things that were not possible become possible.

It is important for teachers of young children to be aware of this phenomenon. For example, many children from their early experiences of multiplying with whole numbers (such as '2 × 3' or '5 × 2') form the idea that multiplication makes things bigger. This would appear to be true in most cases they encounter – three sets of two objects make a set of six, 5 multiplied by 2 becomes 10, and so on. Perhaps their teachers even encourage them in this notion? But this is a false assertion when you come to multiplying by other sorts of numbers. For example,

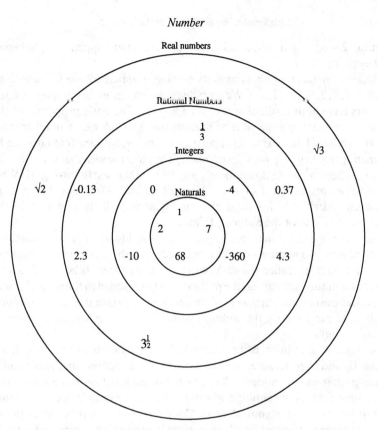

Real numbers

Rational Numbers

$\frac{1}{3}$

Integers

√3

√2   -0.13   0   Naturals   -4   0.37

1

2   7

2.3   -10   68   -360   4.3

$3\frac{1}{2}$

Figure 2.3   A mathematical development of number

if you multiply 4 by 0.1 the answer (0.4) is smaller than the 4 you started with. The problem for us – as teachers – is that these ideas picked up through early experiences of number are very persistent and resistant to change. One 15-year-old girl, tackling a complicated algebraic equation, had correctly simplified it to $10x = 5$. Having demonstrated impressive mathematical skills in attaining this point, she then turned to her teacher and announced that this was stupid because you couldn't multiply 10 by something and get an answer less than 10! The idea that multiplication makes things bigger – which presumably she had picked up when she was about 7 years of age – had persisted through all those years of mathematical experience.

Similar notions are that subtraction makes things smaller and that you cannot subtract a larger number from a smaller number. Many young children these days merrily pressing buttons on calculators are finding for themselves that the second of these assertions is clearly not true! If you haven't done this yourself try entering '2 – 6 =' on a simple calculator and see what happens. So, to begin at the beginning ...

The set of natural numbers consists of those numbers we use for counting: 1, 2, 3, 4, 5, 6, 7, 8, 9, 10, 11, ... We have discussed earlier in this chapter how these numbers have both cardinal and ordinal aspects. The basic properties of these numbers are that there is a starting number (one), then for each number there is a next number. This nextness property is an important idea that children find fascinating, particularly with big numbers. They like the idea that no matter how big a number you write down there's always another one following it! 'What's the next number after forty-six? After fifty-nine? After one hundred and seventeen? After two thousand and ninety-nine?' (All those who said three thousand, like one of the authors, think again!)

The basic operation that can be performed on this set of natural numbers is addition. Any two numbers can be combined using this operation of addition to produce a number, called the sum of the two natural numbers, which is still in the set of natural numbers. So the natural number 2 added to the natural number 4 produces the natural number 6. Mathematicians say that the set is *closed* under addition. In other words, the addition of two natural numbers always produces a natural number.

The *inverse* of addition is the operation known as subtraction. We call it the inverse of addition because, for example, '6 – 2' is defined mathematically as meaning what must be added to 2 to give 6. But the set of natural numbers is not closed under this new operation of subtraction. For example, we cannot find a natural number that is equivalent to '2 – 6'. However, this becomes possible when we extend the set of numbers to include negative numbers and zero. The new set produced by this extension, called the integers, consists of all whole numbers, positive, negative and zero: . . ., –4, –3, –2, –1, 0, 1, 2, 3, 4, ... Note that the set of integers includes the set of natural numbers.

Now that we take 'number' to mean a member of this set of integers, we find that subtraction – which was not previously always possible – becomes always possible. We can always subtract one number from another, for example, '2 – 6 = –4'. But other things have changed as well. For a start we've lost the idea of a first number, since now our set of numbers goes on for ever to the left of zero as well as to the right. So we could no longer say that there's nothing less than 1, or even that there's nothing less than zero. But much more significantly we should note that we have lost the cardinal aspect of number. We can no longer think of numbers as sets of things. We could not demonstrate 2 – 6, for example, by putting out sets of counters and manipulating them in some way. We could, of course, demonstrate it very simply with a number line, as one of our teachers showed with her 5-year-olds in the example quoted earlier in this chapter. This idea that numbers are sets of things, which, as we have seen, so dominates our thinking about number, really doesn't survive for very long in this mathematical development of the concept of number.

The next operation that appears in this development is multiplication. The set of integers is closed under multiplication. In other words, if you multiply one integer by another the result, called the product of the two integers, is an integer, every time. So, for example, the product of 6 and 2 is 12, the product of 6 and –2 (think of six steps of –2 on the number line) is –12. (The explanation of why mathematicians choose to define the product of –2 and –3 to be +6 is abstract, formal, and beyond the scope of this book!)

The inverse of multiplication is the operation known as division. As with the relationship between subtraction and addition, we call this the inverse because, for example, 6 ÷ 2 is defined mathematically as meaning what must be multiplied by 2 to give 6. Now we find that the set of integers is not closed under this new operation of division. We cannot find integers that are equivalent to 2 ÷ 6 or 13 ÷ 5, for example. This then becomes possible by extending the set of numbers to include fractions (and decimals, of course, since decimals, like 0.37 and 4.3 are just fractions, such as 37/100 and 43/10, written in a particular way). The new set produced by this extension is called the set of rational numbers. It consists of all those numbers that are the ratio (hence the word rational) of two integers. For example, 2.3 is a rational number because it is the ratio of 23 to 10, i.e. it is equivalent to 23/10, or 23 ÷ 10. Similarly, 3½ is equivalent to 7/2, –0.13 is equivalent to –13/100, and so on. Note that our set of rational numbers includes the set of integers, which itself included the set of natural numbers. So, for example, –3 is equivalent to –3/1 and 6 is equivalent to 6/1.

We now mean by 'number' a member of the set of all whole numbers, positive, negative or zero, and fractions or decimals. We are now able to label points on the number line between the integers. And we now are always able to divide one number by another – the set of rational numbers is closed under division (with one exception – division by zero is not permissible). We have moved on from the stage where the only ways we can deal with 13 ÷ 5 are by saying 5 doesn't go into 13, or by giving the result as 2 remainder 3. We are now able to state an equivalence between 13 ÷ 5 and the rational number 2.6.

Therefore something that was not always possible is now possible. Other things have changed as well. Suddenly we have lost the nextness property. What is the next number after 2.8? Is it 2.9? How about 2.81? or 2.801? Clearly, there is no next number. An associated gain is that it is now always possible to insert a number between two given numbers. When 'number' meant integer, then we could not always do this. There was no number between 6 and 7, for example. But now that 'number' means rational number, this is always possible. And you can go on and on doing this for ever. This is quite mind-boggling and requires a complete reorganization of our thinking about what numbers are. For any two numbers, it appears that you can go on and on for ever putting more and more numbers in between them.

Young children find some difficulty with the concept of 'between' when applied to numbers, which is not surprising if the cardinal aspect is dominant in their thinking. 'Between' is a spatial concept, and children handle it quite successfully in spatial contexts, such as following an instruction to sit between two individuals. Similarly children can play simple games on a number line involving finding numbers between two given numbers. This is another case where the number line, which is a spatial image of number, helps develop an important concept.

There is yet another extension to the set of numbers, to what mathematicians call the set of real numbers. There are numbers that are not rational (i.e. not exact fractions or decimals) but that nevertheless represent real points on the number line, or real lengths. For example, the length of the diagonal of a square of side one unit is actually equal to the square root of 2 (i.e. $\sqrt{2}$). This is a real number, representing a real length, coming on the number line somewhere between 1.4 and 1.5 or, to be more precise, somewhere between 1.41 and 1.42 or, to be even more precise, somewhere between 1.414213 and 1.414214. But we cannot write down the value of this number exactly in our base-ten, place-value number system. (This means we could not write down a decimal number that, when multiplied by itself, gives the exact answer 2.) All we can say is that it lies between two particular rational numbers. Think of it like this: you can take the bit of the number line between 1 and 2 and divide it up into ten equal parts, and $\sqrt{2}$ will

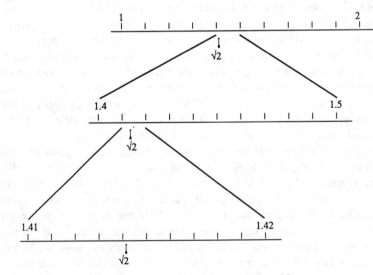

Figure 2.4   Locating the square root of 2

lie between two of the subdivisions, as shown in Figure 2.4. You can then divide this section into ten equal parts and √2 will again lie between two of them. And you can go on and on doing this for ever and ever, dividing the line up into ten equal parts becoming smaller and smaller, and none of your subdivisions will ever land exactly on √2!

Now √2 is not a freak. There are millions of numbers like this, in fact an infinite number of them – the square root of 3, the cube root of 7, and so on – all real numbers in the sense that they represent real points on the number line and real lengths. And yet if they are not rational numbers we cannot actually write them down exactly in our number system! This is quite a dramatic loss, but what we have gained is a continuum of numbers, a complete number line in which every point is associated with a number.

You may well have found the ideas in this last section difficult to understand. In other words, it is difficult to connect them with your existing network of ideas about what numbers are. But we hope that this experience might enable us all to appreciate what it is like for children as their experiences of number are gradually broadened, what it is like to have to come to terms with things that were true becoming false, the false becoming true, the impossible becoming possible and even, in our last step, the possible becoming impossible.

Finally, we would emphasize that this analysis reinforces the view that, even when young children are only at the stage of handling natural numbers, it is important that their activities with number are not limited to those that are relevant only to natural numbers. When other sorts of numbers are encountered later on they will then have some framework of experiences on which to build. In this chapter we have for this reason made much play, for example, on the importance of number-line experiences. In the next two chapters the analysis of number operations, particularly that of subtraction, provides further illustration of this important principle.

SUMMARY OF KEY IDEAS IN CHAPTER 2

1. The concept of a number involves a network of connections between the number symbol, the number name, pictures (such as the number line) and concrete situations (such as sets of counters).

2. There is a potential danger in continually reinforcing just one particular connection in the network of connections constituting a mathematical concept (such as numbers as sets of things) at the expense of equally-important connections (such as numbers as points on a number line), particularly if the connection emphasized is of limited long-term significance.

3. The idea of a number as representing a set of things (e.g. three ducks, five

fingers, ten counters) is called the cardinal aspect of number.

4. Sometimes numbers are used purely as labels (e.g. a number 3 bus). This is called the nominal aspect of number.
5. The idea of number as a label for putting things in order (e.g. page 3, room 9, floor −1) is called the ordinal aspect of number.
6. Counting brings together the cardinal and ordinal aspects of number.
7. Zero does not represent just an empty set (i.e. nothing), but also has, for example, important ordinal meanings, such as a significant point on the number line, the ground floor in a building or freezing point in a temperature scale.
8. The set of natural numbers consists of those numbers used for counting: 1, 2, 3, 4, 5, ...
9. The set of integers comprises all whole numbers, positive, negative or zero: ..., −3, −2, −1, 0, 1, 2, 3, ... The set of integers includes the set of natural numbers.
10. The set of rational numbers consists of all numbers that can be expressed as the ratio of two integers – i.e. all the integers themselves plus all types of fractions, including decimal fractions.
11. A real number is any number representing a point on a number line. The set of real numbers includes the rationals, and also numbers like $\sqrt{2}$ that cannot be written down exactly in our number system, but that nevertheless represents a real point or a real length.
12. Although we cannot write down the exact value of an irrational number in our number system we can specify two rationals between which it lies (e.g. $\sqrt{2}$ lies somewhere between 1.414213 and 1.414214).
13. As the concept of a number develops – through the sets of naturals, integers, rationals, reals – the properties of number change. For example, the cardinality of number is lost in moving from naturals to integers, and the nextness property is lost in moving from integers to rationals.
14. It is important that young children's activities with number should not be limited to those that are only relevant to natural numbers.

SOME ACTIVITIES WITH CHILDREN

Activity 2.1: between

Objective To develop the concept of 'between' in the context of numbers.

Materials A large number line drawn on card, using whatever range of numbers is appropriate for the children concerned; plastic token coins as prizes; a pack of cards with numerals 0–9 written on them; two red and three blue cardboard flags.

Method This is a game for a small group of children. One child, who is confident in using the number line, acts as umpire. The pack of cards is split into two halves, one to generate tens and the other ones. Two cards are turned over by the umpire and a red flag placed at the corresponding point on the number line (e.g. if 2 and 3 are turned over, a flag is placed at 23). Two more cards are turned over and the other red flag positioned.

Players then take it in turn to turn over three pairs of cards. Each pair generates a two-digit number. For each number the child must position a blue flag on the number line. If this is done correctly a penny is awarded by the umpire as a prize. If the blue flag lies *between* the red flags then an extra penny is awarded.

In the example shown in Figure 2.5, the child has correctly positioned flags for 45, 12, and 06, and wins four pennies.

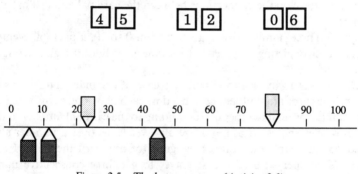

Figure 2.5   The between game (Activity 2.1)

Activity 2.2: I have, who has? (cardinal numbers)

Objective To develop recognition of cardinal numbers.

Materials Prepare a pack of ten cards, with sets of dots on one side and numerals on the other as shown in Figure 2.6. Note that these are arranged so

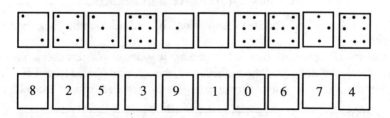

Figure 2.6   Cards for Activity 2.2

that the number of dots on one card corresponds to the numeral on the next, in a continuous cycle.

Method Three children play this version of the game. The cards are shuffled and dealt, the remaining card being placed dots upwards in the centre of the table. The child who has the card with the numeral corresponding to the number of dots displayed places it besides the card in the centre. When all players have agreed that this is correct the card is turned over to reveal the next number to be sought. The first player to get rid of all their cards is the winner. As they play the children should say something along the lines of 'Who has three?' 'I have three . . . . Who has five?' and so on.

Activity 2.3: green bottles

Objective To develop the connections between the cardinal and ordinal aspects of number.

Materials Three number strips labelled from 0 to 10; a pack of twenty-two cards, two each depicting ten green bottles, nine green bottles, eight . . ., one green bottle, blank.

Method This is a game for three children, each of whom has a number strip to work on. The cards are shuffled. One at a time each player turns over a card and places it on the ordinal number corresponding to the cardinal number of the set of green bottles shown. If at any stage a player turns over a number already covered on their strip they can exchange it for any card they wish from an opponent's number strip. The first player to get three consecutive numbers covered as, for example, shown in Figure 2.7, wins the round.

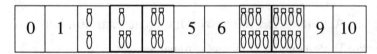

Figure 2.7   Relating cardinal and ordinal numbers in Activity 2.3

Activity 2.4: positive and negative

Objective To extend children's experience of ordinal number into negative integers.

Materials Prepare two dice (write on plain wooden or plastic cubes), one with three faces labelled '+' and three labelled '–', the other numbered from 1 to 6; also required is a number line as shown in Figure 2.8, labelled from –12 to +12, and

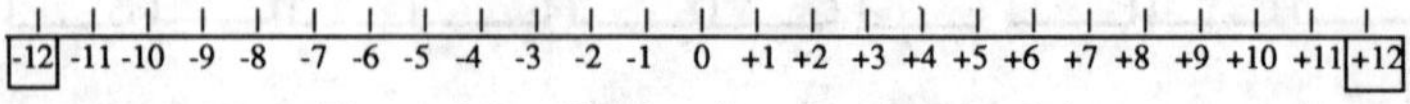

-12 -11 -10 -9 -8 -7 -6 -5 -4 -3 -2 -1 0 +1 +2 +3 +4 +5 +6 +7 +8 +9 +10 +11 +12

Figure 2.8   Number line for Activity 2.4

a coloured counter (or a toy car, etc.) for each player.

Method This is a game for two to four children. To begin with, all their counters are placed on zero. In turn each player throws the two dice and makes the corresponding move on the number line with their counter. For example, if the dice show '–' and '3' then you move three units to the left, and if they show '+' and '3' then you move three units to the right. Every time a player reaches (or passes) +12 or –12 they score a point and return to zero.

Activity 2.5: number displays

Objective To connect together the language, symbols, concrete experiences and pictures of natural numbers.

Materials Anything appropriate that children can find!

Method Make a class display of each natural number from 1 to 10, to which children can add examples from time to time as they come across them. Small groups of children can be given particular responsibility for one display and be encouraged always to be on the lookout for examples of their special number.

For example, the display for 'four' might contain pictures of four people cut from a magazine, or pictures of other sets of four things, such as four legs on a table or an animal, some examples of the written word 'four' cut from newspapers, foreign words for 'four', Roman numerals IV, a birthday card for a 4-year-old, a house number 4, a square, a photograph of a footballer with 4 on his shirt, a number line with 4 highlighted, page 4 from an old book, a clock showing 4 o'clock, a 4 o'clock programme cut from the TV schedules, facts about 4 such as '4 = 3 + 1', '4 = 7 – 3', and so on.

Activity 2.6: root ten

Objective To give young children an opportunity to explore the idea of an irrational number.

Materials A calculator.

Method Children who have some experience of using decimals on calculators might be given the challenge of finding a number that, when multiplied by itself, gives the answer 10. In fact even children as young as 9 or 10 years can make good progress with this investigation. They should keep a record in two columns of the numbers they try that give an answer greater than 10, and the ones that give an answer less than 10, and discover that the number they are looking for always lies between two numbers they can enter on the calculator. For example:

Gives answer < 10	*Gives answer* > 10
3	4
3.1	3.5
3.15	3.25
3.16	3.2
	3.17

and so on ($>$ is the symbol for ' is greater than ' and $<$ is the symbol for ' is less than ').

SUGGESTIONS FOR FURTHER READING

Brown, M. (1986) 'Outdoor negatives', *Mathematics Teaching*. Vol. 114., pp. 14–15. (Brown describes how easily two young children picked up the concept of negative numbers and considers the implications for teaching.)

Carr, K. and Katterns, B. (1984) 'Does the number line help?', *Mathematics in School*, Vol. 13, no. 4, pp. 30–4. (On the basis of experimental work, the authors consider the problems children experience when using a number line. In conclusion they emphasize the need for concrete experience and plenty of discussion work.)

Dickson, L., Brown, M. and Gibson, O. (1984) *Children Learning Mathematics*, Cassell Education for the Schools Council, London. (In section 3 (pp. 169–88) of their book, Dickson and her colleagues discuss the early stages in a child's development of number ideas and the implications for teaching.)

Gelman, R. and Gallistel, C.R. (1978) *The Child's Understanding of Number*, Harvard University Press, Cambridge, Mass., and London. (This book is written by two psychologists who have done extensive work on young children's acquisition and understanding of number concepts. It is intended for all those interested in cognitive development in general and those interested in the foundations of mathematical thought in particular.)

Rotman, B. (1985) 'On zero', *Mathematics Teaching*, Vol. 113, pp. 24–9. (Rotman outlines the history of zero and considers the difficulties its introduction created.)

Schaeffer, B., Eggleston, V.H. and Scott, J.L. (1974) 'Number development in young children', *Cognitive Psychology*, Vol. 6, pp. 208–69. (Basing their conclusions on a study of 65 children between 2 years and 5 years 11 months, Schaeffer and his colleagues describe a four-stage theory of number development.)

Skemp, R.R. (1986) *The Psychology of Learning Mathematics*, Penguin Books, Harmondsworth. (In part B of his book, Skemp explores the meaning of number.)

3
ADD AND SUBTRACT

In this chapter and the next we analyse the concepts of the four operations of addition, subtraction, multiplication and division. We are not concerned here with how to do calculations, but rather with the network of connections that needs to be established for an understanding of what these operations are all about.

WHAT IS ADDITION?

Mark was trying to calculate the number of drinks we would have to provide so that each player in the football tournament could have three drinks during the day. Suddenly he announced a surprising discovery: 'You can use adding for this. I reckon that's why we learn it, so we can use it for things!'

To what sorts of situations can addition be applied? What stories might go with the symbols '12 + 3', for example? 'I've got 12 red pens and 3 blue pens. How many altogether?' 'There are 12 girls and 3 boys. How many children?' Responses like these, clearly interpreting the numbers in the cardinal sense, as sets of things, make use of what we call the *union of two sets* model of addition. Two distinct sets of objects, with no members in common, are put together and the cardinal number of the new set is computed (see Figure 3.1). This is an important model of addition, and one that extends quite easily to other situations where things other than sets are put together: putting two rods end to end to form a train, combining two prices, two weights, two quantities of liquid, and so on, to find out how much altogether.

There is, however, a second model of addition, which we will refer to as *counting on/increasing*. For example, start at 12 and count on 3. This idea

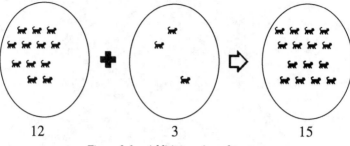

12   3   15

Figure 3.1   Addition: union of two sets

emphasizes the ordinal aspect of the numbers and is experienced most clearly in making moves on a number line (see Figure 3.2).

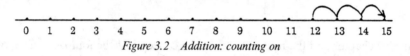

Figure 3.2   Addition: counting on

There are plenty of other situations that are essentially using this model of addition: 'The plant was 12 cm tall, then it grew another 3 cm.' 'The chocolate bar was 12p last week, but now the price has gone up by 3p.' Although we have talked about these as two different models of addition there is, nevertheless, a clear relationship between them. In fact, connecting the two models together is an important stage in the development of a child's understanding of addition. This is the point at which the child is able to apply the process of counting on, in order to find out how many altogether in the union of two sets, rather than counting the complete set from 1. Counting on using the number line is an important facilitator in this development.

On the whole, then, most children find it not too difficult to connect together the concrete situations and pictures that go with the language and symbols of addition. But this is certainly not the case when it comes to subtraction, which is a much more complex affair altogether.

WHAT IS SUBTRACTION?

Mary, a bright 7-year-old, had written down these calculations:

$$9 - 3 = 5$$
$$12 - 4 = 7$$
$$15 - 6 = 8$$
$$14 - 10 = 3$$
$$10 - 7 = 2$$

Her teacher talked to her about what she had done:

TEACHER. Now, Mary, what sort of sums are these?

MARY Takes.

TEACHER. What's this first one say then?

MARY. 9 take 3?

TEACHER. 9 take away 3. What's the answer for 9 take away 3?

MARY [*Looking at her answer*]. Five. No, that's wrong, it's 6.

TEACHER. Well, what about this one? 12 take away 4?

MARY. Seven?

TEACHER [*Putting out 12 cubes*]. Show me 12 take away 4.

MARY [*Manipulating the cubes*]. 1, 2, 3, 4. That leaves 1, 2, 3, 4, 5, 6, 7, 8. Eight.

TEACHER. How did you get 7?

MARY [*Pointing to a number line at the top the page in her textbook*]. I did it on this. Look. [*She puts her finger on the 12 on the number line and counts back 4 until it rests on the 8*] There you are, it's 7!

TEACHER [*Pointing to Mary's finger resting on the 8*]. Why isn't the answer 8?

MARY. Because I've taken that one away.

TEACHER. Well, show me 9 take away 3 then.

[*Mary carries out the same procedure on the number line, until her finger rests on the 6*]

MARY. It's 5. [*Looks puzzled*]

TEACHER. But why isn't it 6? You're pointing to the 6.

MARY. No, it must be 5, because I've taken the 6 away.

TEACHER. So what do you really think is the answer for 9 take away 3?

MARY. 6.

The above dialogue illustrates just how potentially difficult it is to make valid connections between the different models of subtraction, and also highlights a significant point about language that will emerge in the subsequent analysis of this concept.

First, we should ask to what sort of situations can subtraction be applied? What stories could we write to go with, say, '12 – 3'? Some teachers' responses:

- There are 12 birds sitting on a fence. Then 3 fly away. How many still on the fence?
- There are 12 trees in a forest and an elephant knocks over 3 of them. How many trees left standing?
- I had 12 chocolates and ate 3 of them. How many left for tomorrow?

These stories all have basically the same plot. It is what we will call the *partitioning* model (see Figure 3.3). We find that most students and teachers, when asked to write a story for subtraction, produce a version of this plot. There's a set of 12 things and somehow 3 of them are partitioned off, taken away, removed, eaten, destroyed, lost, blown up, stolen, given away or mortally wounded. In each case the question posed is, essentially, how many are left?

All these stories use the cardinal aspect of number, but similar plots can be written with numbers used for measuring, where the question posed will be, essentially, how much left? 'I had 12p and I spent 3p. How much did I have left?' 'There were 12 litres of wine in my cellar. We drank 3 litres. How much wine is left in my cellar now?' As with most mathematical symbols, we find that '12 – 3'

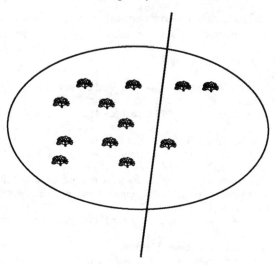

Figure 3.3 Subtraction: partitioning

may be connected to a wide range of very different situations. Subtraction is by no means just the partitioning plot. It is not just a synonym for 'take away'. Partitioning is just one model of subtraction, and a very limited one at that.

The following stories written by children for '12 – 3' illustrate five different models of subtraction, and therefore some of the connections that have to be made to develop a fuller understanding of the concept (children's spelling retained):

1. There were 12 books on the pile. The teacher took 3 of them away. How many left?
2. If my friend is 12 and his brother is 3 how older is he?
3. There were 12 soldiers 3 were ill how many were not ill?
4. The price of a choc bar was 12p the shop thought it was deer and took 3p off.
5. Jhon was 3 and 9 year latter he was 12.

Story (1) uses the familiar and most-frequently used partitioning model with the associated 'take away, how many left?' language. Story (2) introduces another and very important aspect of subtraction, what we will call the *comparison* model. In this story the basic plot is that the two numbers 12 and 3 are compared. A line of 12 blue cubes is compared with a line of 3 red cubes (see Figure 3.4). A price of 12p is compared with a price of 3p. A weight of 12 kg is compared with a weight of 3 kg. Notice one significant difference between this model and partitioning. Both the 12 and the 3 are there right from the start. In partitioning you start with the 12, and the 3 you take away is part of the 12. Here you have the 12 and the 3 side by side and you compare them.

There are three versions of the punch-line in stories with the comparison plot.

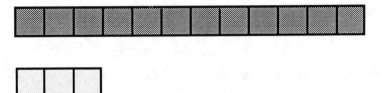

Figure 3.4   Subtraction: comparison

The child who produced story (2) asked 'how older is he?' presumably meaning 'how much older?' Equally the question could have been 'how much younger?' or 'what is the difference in their ages?' Similarly, when comparing two sets we may ask 'how many more in A?' or 'how many less in B?' or 'what is the difference between A and B?' (Some people may prefer the word 'fewer' to 'less' in this context, but it seems to us that this use of this word is disappearing from the vernacular.)

'Difference' is used here in a technical mathematical sense. We do not mean, for example, that the difference between the red cubes and the blue cubes in Figure 3.4 is their colour! We should note that the difference between 3 and 12 is the same as the difference between 12 and 3, but '3 – 12' is not the same as '12 – 3'. Notice also the interpretation of 'difference between' on the number line, as illustrated in Figure 3.5, where '12 – 3' is represented by the gap between 12 and 3. This is a powerful image of subtraction and one that is often used in mental calculations – many people, when calculating '105 – 78' mentally, for example, would deal with it essentially by adding together the bits needed to fill the gap between 78 and 105, namely '5 + 2 + 20' (in various orders).

We want to emphasize at this point how different are the actual manipulations of, say, cubes on a table, when using the partitioning and the comparison models. In the first instance, you put out a set of 12 cubes and take 3 of them away. In the second case you put out a set of 12 cubes and a set of 3 cubes and compare them. Yet both manipulations correspond to the symbols '12 – 3'. Comparing two sets or quantities to find out how many more or how many less is just as valid and important an interpretation of subtraction as taking something away from a set or quantity.

The language of comparison merits some special consideration. When we make a comparison between two quantities, using subtraction, there are always

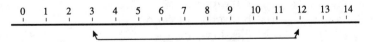

Figure 3.5   The difference between 12 and 3

two equivalent ways of stating the relationship, two sets of language available. Mathematically this is expressed by the statement

$$A > B \text{ is equivalent to } B < A.$$

So on the one hand there is the language that focuses on the larger quantity:

A is more than B
A is greater than B
A is larger than B
A is bigger than B
A is taller than B
A is higher than B
A is longer than B
A is further than B
A is wider than B
A is fatter than B
A is heavier than B
A holds more than B
A costs more than B
A takes longer than B
A is later than B
A is older than B
A is faster than B

and so on.

On the other hand, there is the language that focuses on the smaller quantity:

B is less than A
B is smaller than A
B is shorter than A
B is lower than A
B is nearer than A
B is narrower than A
B is thinner than A
B is lighter than A
B holds less than A
B costs less than A
B takes less time than A
B is earlier than A
B is younger than A
B is slower than A

and so on.

It is an interesting observation that in practice, when we make comparisons, in most situations we tend to use language from the first list – language that makes the greater quantity the subject of the sentence. A child will complain 'It's not fair, he's got more than me', but never 'I've got less than him!' Inevitably the one with more becomes the focus of attention. It is significant that we actually have more words in everyday language to express the greater aspect than we do to express the smaller one, as can be seen from the lists above. It is also significant that the last sentence was automatically written using the word 'more' with the longer list as the subject, when it could equally well have been written as 'we actually have less words in everyday language to express the smaller aspect'. In order to build up connections with the full range of language, teachers asking pupils to make comparisons need to make a conscious effort to use 'more' no more than they use 'less' or, to put it another way, to use 'less' no less than they use 'more'. In fact we would advocate that we make it a rule that whenever children make a comparison they have to make the two equivalent statements. So if they have observed that a pencil costs 3p more than a ballpoint, they should immediately be encouraged to make the equivalent observation that the ballpoint costs 3p less than the pencil. If measuring leads to the discovery that Reuben is 3 cm taller than Rachel, then we also make a sentence beginning 'Rachel is ...'.

There is a subtle problem built into the concept of 'less than' that makes it considerably more difficult for a child to handle than 'more than'. This is illustrated by a teacher's account of an interaction with a 7-year-old:

I put 2 sweets in my hand and 5 in Clare's. She seemed to understand that she had more than me. I asked how many more did she have. She said she had 5 more. That seemed a reasonable response – although not the one I was looking for – since she did have 5 and she did have more. We did the obvious thing of laying our sweets out on the table and matching them, so that the 3 more in her pile could be identified. She quickly cottoned on to the idea that she had 3 more than me. We did a few more examples like this and she handled 'more than' with considerable success. I then put 2 sweets in her hand and 5 in mine. With a bit of prompting she managed to say that she had less than me. I then asked her how many less. This completely defeated her, even when we laid out our sweets and matched them. The best she could manage was 'I've got 2 more less than you'. I then realized what a difficult task I had set Clare. I wanted her to look at the 2 sweets in her hand and make a statement beginning with the words 'I've got 3 ...' (I've got 3 less than you). But she didn't have those 3, I had them!

The point to note here is that when we use subtraction in this comparison model to make statements of the form '3 is 9 less than 12' we appear to be making a statement about the 3, since we begin with the words '3 is ...', but in fact the 9 is actually part of the 12. This underlines the importance of establishing the

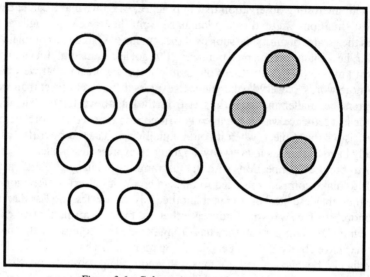

Figure 3.6   Subtraction: complement of a set

equivalence of two statements like 'I have 3 more than you' and 'You have 3 less than me'.

Story (3) uses what we call the *complement of a set* model (see Figure 3.6). The basic plot is that there is a set of 12 things, 3 of which have some attribute. The question posed is how many do not have this attribute. The word 'not' is usually central to the punch-line of stories with this plot. This model is fairly similar to partitioning and it would seem to be not too difficult for children to learn to apply the same symbols and arithmetic process to these two models.

Story (4) uses what we call the *counting back/reducing* model. It is clearly the reverse of the counting on/increasing model of addition. The basic plot in this case is that you start at the 12 and count back or reduce the quantity by 3. A 12-stones person losing 3 stones of weight after dieting would be using this model. The most important picture of this model of subtraction and, therefore, an important experience for children, is counting back (or down) along the number line (see Figure 3.7).

Finally, there is a fifth model of subtraction, illustrated by the story by child (5): we call this the *inverse of addition* model. In many ways this would appear to be the most important and fundamental model of subtraction. As is seen in

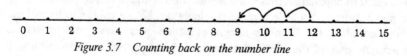

Figure 3.7   Counting back on the number line

Chapter 2, from a mathematical point of view subtraction is defined as the inverse of addition. In this model the plot becomes 'What must be added to 3 to make 12?' The remarkable thing about story (5) is that it actually begins with the 3. The child who made up this story has clearly interpreted '12 – 3' as meaning

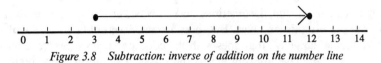

Figure 3.8   Subtraction: inverse of addition on the number line

that you start at the 3 and add on until you arrive at 12, as illustrated on the number line in Figure 3.8.

Some structural apparatus emphasizes this model of subtraction. For example, with colour-factor rods, '12 – 3' can become a question of finding which rod has to be added to the 3-rod to make a train the same length as the 12-rod (see Figure 3.9). Once again we want to emphasize how significantly different from other models is the manipulation of materials involved in this model of

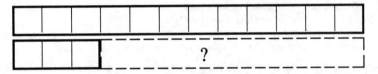

Figure 3.9   Inverse of addition with structural apparatus

subtraction. Earlier we were putting out a set of 12 cubes and taking away 3, then we were putting out sets of 12 and 3 cubes and comparing them, and now we would be putting out 3 cubes and adding on until we arrive at 12. Yet all these – partitioning, comparison, inverse of addition, as well as complement of a set and counting back – are situations to which the subtraction symbol has to be connected. They are all part of the complex network of connections that constitute the concept of subtraction. This is a most dramatic example of the way in which one symbol is used in mathematics to represent many different and varied situations.

As with the cardinal aspect of number, we have again the potential problem of one connection being emphasized too strongly in the early years of schooling at the expense of other, equally-important connections. Infant teachers may focus on the take-away interpretation of subtraction almost to the exclusion of other models. This is only one model of subtraction, and a very limited one. Yet when teachers set out to demonstrate a subtraction question to children they almost invariably put out a set of objects and take some away. The comparison and inverse of addition models are, in the long run, much more significant models, yet too many children (and teachers) seem fixated on the take-away model.

- I think I've just seen the light! I always used to think that "–" meant "take away". But it doesn't, does it? It means lots of other things as well.
- But we always say "take away" when we write the symbol down.

Of course, subtraction is sometimes 'take away', and when this is so it is appropriate to use this language. But there are two levels of language involved here, the formal language that goes with the concept, such as 'twelve subtract three' and the language appropriate to the physical situation. This might be 'twelve take away three', but it might be 'twelve count back three', or the language of comparison, and so on. The problem that Mary encountered in the dialogue quoted at the start of this section would appear to be related to the fact that she is saying and thinking 'take away' when she is not using the take-away model, but counting back.

Later on in their mathematical careers, children are going to encounter calculations like '6 – (–3) = ?' What do you make of this?

M. I know the answer's 9, but I don't understand why.
C. It's because two minuses make a plus.
D. Why do you smile when you say that?
C. I suppose it's because I know it's no explanation really. It's just a trick or a rule someone taught me. I've no idea what it means or why it works!

Most people feel very uneasy about a statement like '6 – (–3) = 9'. This is not surprising in view of the dominance of 'take away' in our understanding of subtraction. If you say to yourself 'six take away negative three' then you will probably imagine a pile of six objects and wonder what on earth taking away negative three of them could mean. We must assume, of course, that –3 itself has some meaning for us. Let's connect it, for example, with a temperature (or a lift button, or your bank balance, whichever is closest to your experience). Now connect the symbols '6 – (–3)' with a temperature situation, using the comparison model, for example. Does this suddenly make sense? If the temperature inside is 6 degrees and the temperature outside is –3 degrees, then ...? Or connect the symbols with the number line, using the inverse of addition model. If you start at –3, what do you have to add to get to 6?

So what is the teacher's task in developing understanding of subtraction? It would appear to be a question of helping the child to build up a network of connections between the symbols and the various models that have been outlined in the above analysis:

> partitioning
> comparison
> complement of a set
> counting back/reducing
> inverse of addition

and then to operate on concrete and real situations:

> sets of objects
> coins
> prices
> lengths
> ages

and so on; and on the picture of number in the number line; and to connect all this with the language of subtraction, both the formal word 'subtract' and the range of language appropriate to the various actual physical situations, particularly the language of comparison.

That's quite an agenda! And we have not even considered the problems of doing the sums. Perhaps we should be grateful for the emergence of inexpensive calculators, so that we can concentrate on building up the children's understanding and leave the calculator's electronic circuits to do all the tedious, routine calculations. Certainly it is more and more the case that knowing what calculation to do in a given situation is more important than just being able to do the calculation. In the future we suspect that the basic question of arithmetic is going to be 'Which buttons do you press on the calculator to answer this problem?'

So how will understanding be recognized? By the child demonstrating that connections between the concrete situations, symbols, language and pictures of subtraction are being established. By showing us what the symbols '12 – 3' mean in terms of a set of counters, or two sticks of cubes placed side by side, or on a number line. By being able to make up number stories using more than one model of subtraction, like the stories (1), (2), (3), (4) and (5) cited above. By knowing what sum to do on a calculator – for a take-away situation; for finding out how many are not; for counting back or reducing; for comparing two numbers to find out how many more or how many less; and for determining what must be added to one number to give another.

SUMMARY OF KEY IDEAS IN CHAPTER 3

1. Two categories of situations to which the language and symbols of addition can be connected are the union of two sets (with no members in common), and counting on/increasing.
2. Five categories of situations to which the language and symbols of subtraction can be connected are partitioning, complement of a set, counting back/reducing, comparison and inverse of addition.
3. Particularly important in understanding subtraction is the language of comparison.

4. For any comparison statement that makes the greater quantity the subject of the sentence there is an equivalent statement that makes the smaller quantity the subject.

5. Subtraction is not just 'take away'. This language applies only to partitioning, which is a limited model of subtraction. It cannot be applied, for example, to situations involving negative numbers.

SOME ACTIVITIES WITH CHILDREN

Activity 3.1: stories (addition, subtraction)

Objective To help children connect the symbols for addition and subtraction with a wide range of situations and language.

Method Read the children some examples of stories for addition statements, such as '3 + 5'. Get them to make up their own stories, writing them down or even tape-recording them, for examples such as '4 + 8' or '9 − 3'. Use larger numbers if appropriate. Children should share their stories with each other and discuss their validity.

Then, to encourage the use of different models and contexts, give specific words or phrases to be included in the story, such as 'more than', 'less than', 'increased', 'reduced', 'younger', 'older'. Alternatively, give the children the start of the story and ask them to complete it. For example, for '9 − 3': 'Mary had 9 marbles, but Tom only had ...'.

Activity 3.2: swaps (addition and subtraction)

Objective To develop connections between language, symbols, concrete experience and pictures, for the concepts of addition and subtraction.

Materials Coins, 1p and 10p; base-ten materials, longs and units; number lines; a calculator; blank paper; a collection of simple stories for addition and subtraction; cards with the following words written on them: story, number line, picture, calculator, symbols, coins, blocks.

Method A small group of children is given a starting-point and a selection of cards indicating a sequence of swaps to be achieved. When they have completed all their swaps they report on what they have done to the teacher.

Figure 3.10 shows an example with a story given as the starting-point, and a challenge in this case to swap this for coins, a calculator sum, then for a number-line drawing and finally for symbols. The children might respond to this challenge by putting out 8p and a further 4p to make the 12p required, enter '8 + 4 =' or even '12 − 8 =' on their calculator, draw an arrow on a number line from 8 to 12 and finally write on their piece of paper the symbols '8 + 4 = 12' or '12

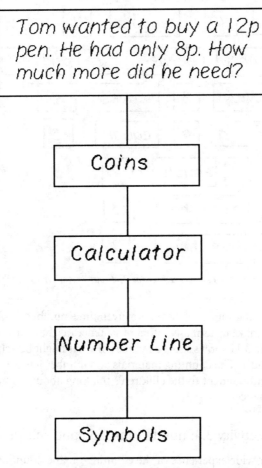

Figure 3.10 Swaps (Activity 3.2)

$-8 = 4$'. The starting-point may be a story, a number-line diagram, a sum written in symbols or a picture, and the sequence of swaps varied appropriately.

Activity 3.3: sentences (addition and subtraction)

Objective To develop language patterns for addition and subtraction.

Materials Several sets of strips of card with the following words or phrases written on them – add, subtract, and, take away, more than, less than, the difference, between, makes, leaves, is, equals – and several sets of cards with appropriate numerals and signs written on them; counting materials and a number line.

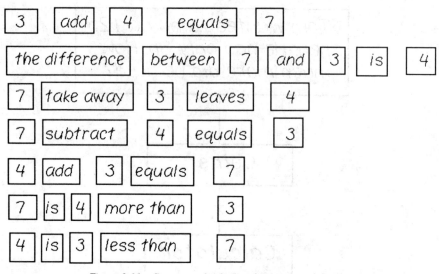

Figure 3.11   Sentences for 3, 4 and 7 (Activity 3.3)

Method A small group of children are given three numbers and challenged to use the cards to make up as many different sentences as they can using these three numbers. Figure 3.11 shows some examples of what might be achieved with the numbers 3, 4 and 7. The counting materials and number line are simply used to give concrete embodiment to the children's thinking about the numbers and to check their sentences.

Activity 3.4: number line add and subtract

Objective To provide experience of the counting-on and counting-back models of addition and subtraction in the context of a number line.

Materials Two conventional dice numbered from 1 to 6; a counter (or an appropriate small toy); a number line marked from 0 to 12; a small flag of some sort. (For a more advanced game, use dodecahedra dice with faces numbered from 1 to 12, and a number line marked from 0 to 24.)

Method This is a simple game for a small group of players. The player going first places the flag on the number line on any number of their choosing. Each then plays in turn as follows. They place the counter on the zero mark, throw the first die and move the counter to this number. Throw the second die and *predict* which number they will finish on when they have moved this number of places. They then move and, if correct, win a point. If they finish on the number with the flag on they receive a bonus point.

A subtraction version can also be played, in which the counter starts on 12 and moves are made towards zero. This time they have to predict which number they will land on after each throw of the dice, so it is possible to win three points on each turn: one for the first prediction, one for the second and one if they finish up on the flagged number.

Activity 3.5: what did I do? (12,+,– version)

Objective To give children experience of addition and subtraction as inverses of each other.

Materials One calculator per two children; plastic pennies as prizes.

Method Players take it in turns to challenge each other with the question 'What did I do?' The number 12 is entered on the calculator. Player A presses either '+' or '–', followed by a single digit and the equals key. The calculator is then shown to player B who has to (1) state which keys A pressed, and (2) press either '+' or '–', followed by a single digit and the equals key, in order to get the 12 back on display. B wins one penny for correctly stating which keys A pressed, and a further penny for getting back to 12. It is then player B's turn to challenge A.

An interesting discussion might ensue if, after performing an operation, the first player hands the calculator to the second player with 12 still on display.

Activity 3.6: more than/less than

Objective To strengthen understanding of 'more than', 'less than', and to link these ideas with 'take away' and 'difference'.

Materials 40 Unifix cubes, 20 each of two colours, say, blue and orange; 20 cards, 10 each saying 'more than' and 'less than'; two pots or boxes.

Method This is a game for two children plus a third acting as umpire. Each player has 20 cubes of one colour to start with. The pack of cards is placed face down on the table. Players play in turn as follows.

One player stands any number of cubes, joined together, on the table, stating how many have been played. (The first player in each turn must play two or more cubes, unless there is only one left.) The second player than plays any number of cubes different from the first. The top card is turned over. If it says 'more than' the player who has played more than the other wins. Similarly, if it says 'less than' the one playing less wins.

The winning player actually wins the difference between the two columns of cubes. These cubes are then taken from the larger pile and placed in the winner's pot. The equal residues are then returned to the players and the game continues, until both players' supply of cubes is reduced to one. These remaining single cubes are put into the pots.

The object of the game is to get the most cubes into your pot. These may be cubes of either colour.

Note On a 'less-than' card you win cubes from the other person's pile, but on a 'more-than' card the winnings come from your own pile. The umpire's job is to insist that the players say the appropriate words at each stage and to check on fair play. They must say, for example, 'I play ... cubes', when making their play. And the winner each time must use correctly the words written on the card (i.e. 'more than' or 'less than') and the word 'difference', for example, 'My 2 is less than your 5, and the difference is 3'. If they don't do this then they forfeit their winnings.

A variation is to give each player one pound in small change instead of cubes.

Activity 3.7: I have, who has? (addition and subtraction stories)

Objective To practise using all the models and language for addition and subtraction.

Materials Prepare a set of 16 cards with 'questions' on one side and the corresponding 'answers' on the other side, using the same cyclic scheme as explained in Activity 2.2, with the question on one card answered on the reverse side of the next.

This time use as questions a series of statements or stories covering the whole range of models and language for addition and subtraction. Here are some suggestions, with the corresponding answers in brackets after each one:

1. Start at 4 and count on 7. (4 + 7)
2. John has 3 apples, Peter has 8. How many more than John has Peter? (8 – 3)
3. Jill had 8 apples. She ate 5. How many left? (8 – 5)
4. Twelve subtract seven. (12 – 7)
5. The difference between 4 and 7. (7 – 4)
6. Eight add four. (8 + 4)
7. A 7p pencil went up by 5p. What does it now cost? (7 +5)
8. A 12p choc bar was reduced by 5p. What does it now cost? (12 – 5)
9. I want to buy a book costing £7. I only have £3. How much more do I need? (7 – 3)
10. John is 4, Jack is 8. How much younger is John? (8 – 4)
11. Start at 12 and count back 8. (12 – 8)
12. There are 12 children. If 4 are going on a school trip, how many are not going? (12 – 4)
13. One sweet costs 4p, another costs 3p. How much for them both? (4 + 3)
14. The sum of 7 and 4. (7 + 4)

15. I am 12. How old was I three years ago? (12 − 3)
16. How many less than 8 is 7? (8 − 7)

Method The cards are shuffled and dealt between the players, with the remaining card placed in the centre of the table. The game is then played in exactly the same way as in Activity 2.2.

SUGGESTIONS FOR FURTHER READING

Brown, J.S. and Burton, R.B. (1978) 'Diagnostic models for procedural "bugs" in basic mathematical skills', *Cognitive Science*, Vol. 2, pp. 155–92. (The authors of this paper analysed the errors made by 2,500 children and concluded that, in most cases, the child has followed some well-defined procedure that was in general identical to the 'correct' procedure except for one or more faulty steps.)

Carpenter, T.P., Moser, J.M. and Romberg, T.A. (eds.) (1982) *Addition and Subtraction: A Cognitive Perspective*, Lawrence Erlbaum Associates, Hillsdale, NJ. (This book provides a wide variety of readings written by eminent mathematicians and psychologists from all over the world.)

Hebbler, K. (1981) 'Young children's addition', in A. Floyd (ed.) *Developing Mathematical Thinking*, Addison-Wesley in association with the Open University, Wokingham. (This short paper describes a study designed to examine the quantitive problem-solving processes of children in the pre- and early years of schooling.)

Hughes, M. (1986) *Children and Number*, Blackwell, Oxford. (In Chapter 3 of his book, Hughes describes young children's understanding of the concepts of addition and subtraction prior to schooling. In subsequent chapters he considers the difficulties created by the formal demands of schooling.)

Kamii, C. (1985) *Young Children Reinvent Arithmetic*, Teachers' College Press, New York, NY. (In Part II (Chapters 5 and 6) of her book, Kamii discusses the skills that a young child needs to appreciate the concepts of addition and subtraction and how such understanding may best be acquired.)

4
MULTIPLY AND DIVIDE

A similar analysis of multiplication and division to that of addition and subtraction is undertaken in this chapter. It is as well for teachers of young children to have a clear understanding of the network of connections that will eventually need to be established for some understanding of what these operations are about, even though their pupils may only be at the stage of handling them informally. To help in this analysis we make extensive use of stories written by 9–11-year-old children to go with multiplication and division statements. Although these are children a little older than many of those whose teachers are being addressed in this book, these stories nevertheless provide a number of significant insights into the confusions that might arise from the ways in which younger children might first encounter the operations and symbols of multiplication and division.

WHAT IS MULTIPLICATION?

The following are typical of the responses obtained when 9–11-year-old children are asked to write a story for 9 × 3:

- 9 and 3 stood in a shop they said please could we have a times sign. He said yes so they walked along with the times sign in the middle.
- Belinda could not work out 9 × 3 because it was too hard for her.
- 9 children were writing an essay and 3 more children joined them. That made 27 children altogether.
- The boy had 9 pens and the teacher asked him what would 9 × 3 be. He said 27 and the teacher said that's right.
- 9 said to 3 lets multiply together and see what it makes.

Very few children seem to have a clear model in their mind of what multiplication means, even when they apparently know their tables and can recall multiplication facts like '9 × 3 = 27' with confidence. It seems as though multiplication is something you do with numbers in mathematics lessons in school, but is not connected with any confidence to the real world. For many children a multiplication statement is just a set of marks made on a piece of paper, which is either right or wrong, or an instruction to recall the appropriate response, which you can either do or not do. So how do infant teachers interpret multiplication?

- I must admit I just think of it as 9 times 3, something you do with numbers.
- It's nine sets of three isn't it?
- Or is it three sets of nine?
- No, surely that would be 3 times 9?
- I don't think it matters, it's both, isn't it?

Certainly one important category of situations to which multiplication must be connected is that to which these teachers are alluding: the idea that the multiplication sign means 'sets of'. This can be referred to as the *repeated addition* model of multiplication, since it uses 3 sets of 9, for example, and is connected also with '9 + 9 + 9'. Of course, this model is appropriate in these terms only to cardinal numbers, where the second number is the number of objects in a set and the first is the number of these sets.

But there is a question here that causes some confusion and that we should try to sort out. Does '9 × 3' mean 'nine sets of three' or 'three sets of nine'? Which of the pictures (a) or (b) in Figure 4.1 should be connected with these symbols? The first thing to note is that it is by no means immediately obvious that nine sets of three objects and three sets of nine objects come to the same result. The two diagrams in Figure 4.1 do not immediately strike one as necessarily representing the same number. The fact that they do is an instance of the property of multiplication known as *commutativity*. Formally this is the rule that says that '$a \times b$' is always equal to '$b \times a$', whatever the two numbers a and b.

The other operation for which commutativity holds is, of course, addition, since $a + b = b + a$, for any two numbers a and b. There is a stage in their development of understanding of addition in which young children gradually acquire the idea that a set of five objects combined with a set of four objects is the same as a set of four combined with a set of five. At least with addition there does not appear to be much perceptual difference between, say, holding up four fingers on your left hand and five on your right hand, and holding up five fingers on your left and four on your right. Although there is a transformation involved between the two situations, the equivalence is clearly apparent. Eventually most children are able to switch freely between, say, '5 + 4' and '4 + 5'. But this is much more of a hurdle for multiplication. The equivalence between four sets of five

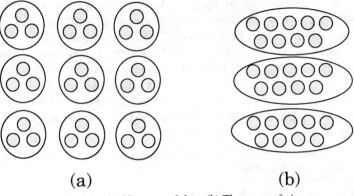

(a)   **(b)**

Figure 4.1   (a) Nine sets of three (b) Three sets of nine

and five sets of four is not clearly apparent, and many children would find the calculation of one much more difficult than the calculation of the other.

Now, strictly speaking, the words 'nine times three' mean that you have nine, three times. In other words, 'nine times three' is 'three sets of nine', as shown in Figure 4.1 (b). Similarly, the formal language 'nine multiplied by three' also refers to the picture in Figure 4.1 (b): a set of nine is reproduced three times. So in this strict interpretation, '9 × 3' represents '9 + 9 + 9', whereas '3 × 9' represents '3 + 3 + 3 + 3 + 3 + 3 + 3 + 3 + 3'.

Some primary textbooks take this very seriously and formally, and take children through the sequence

$$3 \text{ sets of } 9 = 3(9) = 9 \times 3 = 27.$$

We would not wish to be as formal or as pedantic as this. In fact, it would seem to us to be appropriate that the commutative nature of multiplication be established before the introduction of the formal representation in symbols. Then when the multiplication sign is introduced it really would be the case that both '9 × 3' and '3 × 9' could represent either nine sets of three or three sets of nine.

In order to establish commutativity it is most helpful if considerable attention is given to connecting one particular picture of multiplication into the network of experiences associated with this concept. This is the picture of a *rectangular array*, as shown in Figure 4.2(a) and (b). It is our contention that pictures such as these should form a major component of our understanding of '9 × 3'. One of the reasons for this emphasis on the notion of rectangular array is that this picture of multiplication makes the commutative property much more immediately apparent. So Figure 4.2 (a) can be talked about as being both 'nine rows of three dots' (going across the page) and 'three rows of nine dots' (going

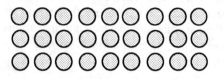

(a) **(b)**

Figure 4.2 Rectangular arrays for '9 × 3'

down the page). Clearly, in this case nine threes and three nines are the same. Later on, then, both '9 × 3' or '3 × 9' can be used as symbols to represent these diagrams.

Young children, before they start recording multiplication facts such as '3 × 4 = 12' formally, can be encouraged to identify rectangular arrays in their environment – the western world is full of them – and to record their observations with a diagram and an appropriate comment, as in Figure 4.3.

We are beginning to see again that understanding of a number operation is involving the establishment of a network of connections. Understanding multiplication would seem to involve connecting the language of 'multiplied by' and 'times', concrete situations such as repeated sets of objects, the symbols for

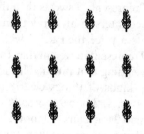

3 rows of 4 trees

three fours make twelve

Figure 4.3 Recording arrays

multiplication statements and the important picture of the rectangular array. With this picture forming a major component of the multiplication network the child has something to which to connect later experiences in mathematics, such as finding areas of rectangles using multiplication.

The question we must consider now is whether the idea that '9 × 3' means '3 sets of 9' is the only model for multiplication, or do we face a similar situation to that with addition and subtraction, where the symbols and the language had to be connected to a number of different categories of experiences? So, can we recall other situations in which multiplication is the appropriate operation, other occasions in real life in which we might press the multiplication key on the calculator?

- We use it a lot when we're shopping, don't we. When you're working out the cost of 3 things at 9p each, for example.
- But isn't that just three sets of nine again?
- Not really. Nine pence isn't necessarily a set of nine things.
- And what about 3 lengths of 9 cm, or 3 periods of 9 minutes, or 3 buckets each containing 9 litres?

We can now see that the repeated addition model, which has so far been thought of as repeated sets, has to be extended to other contexts, such as money, length, weight, capacity, time, and so on. Each of the ideas suggested above in these various contexts has to be connected with '9 × 3' or '3 × 9'. This is a not too-difficult extension of the repeated addition model, but we should note that now only one of the numbers is a cardinal number, representing the number of things in a set, and the other number is used for measuring a length or a value or a weight, and so on.

This highlights one of the inbuilt difficulties in interpreting multiplication in concrete terms, namely that the two numbers must represent different sorts of things. So if the 9 in '9 × 3' represents 9 sweets then the 3 will represent bags of sweets. If the 9 represents counters in an array then the 3 represents rows of counters. If the 9 represents a price then the 3 will represent the number of articles at that price. If the 9 represents a weight then the 3 represents the number of individual things each weighing that much. This idea that the two numbers have to represent different kinds of things clearly throws some children, as illustrated in some of their stories. 'I had 9 footballs and I lost 3 footballs, then I got back 3 footballs, so I had 9 footballs × 3 footballs.' 'The army had 9 tanks and the navy had 3 ships. When they timesed them together they were the biggest army in the whole world.'

There is actually a further model of multiplication to be considered. We might call this the *scaling* model, in which a quantity is scaled by a factor. This model is used in the following story, for example: 'I have 3 pens. My friend has 9 times as many. How many has she got?' At a casual glance the reader may well think this is no different from the repeated addition model. But we should note that we are not dealing here with 'nine sets of three pens', but with two sets of pens, and the '9 times as many' is used to express a relationship between them.

This scaling model of multiplication is an important component of the network of connections because of later mathematical experiences involving this idea of scaling. So, for example, it might be used when calculating a percentage increase, or when dealing with scale factors in mapwork and scale drawings.

WHAT IS DIVISION?

What image comes most readily to our minds when we see the symbols '12 ÷ 3'? If I put twelve cubes on the desk what would you expect me to do with them to demonstrate '12÷3'?

- I expect you to share them into three piles. One for you, one for you and one for you. And so on.
- So the answer is how many in each pile. What do you say when you have done this?
- Twelve shared by three is four.
- Twelve shared between three is four each, surely.
- I think I sometimes just say twelve share three is four, but I don't think it's right to say that.
- I was thinking of something different. I had in mind sharing the twelve cubes into piles of three.
- And if you do that where's the answer?
- It's the number of piles you finish up with.
- So twelve divided by three is also how many threes in twelve?
- I'd never think of it like that. I'd only think of it as sharing between three.

We are back on familiar ground. The elementary mathematical operation of division, represented by the symbol ÷, appears to represent more than one type of situation, as has been the case with all the mathematical symbols we have analysed so far. On the one hand, the symbols '12 ÷ 3' are connected to the idea of sharing twelve between three. A set of twelve objects would thus be arranged into three groups, as shown in Figure 4.4(a), and the answer is the number of objects in each group. We will call this the *sharing* model. But just as valid is to interpret '12 ÷ 3' as 'how many threes make 12?' In this *inverse of multiplication* model, the twelve objects are arranged into groups of three, as shown in Figure 4.4 (b), and the answer is the number of groups.

- I'm not sure I ever really realized that division could mean two different things like that! I always think of it as sharing.
- What's 72 divided by 9?
- (After some thought) Eight.
- What went on in your mind when you worked that out?
- I was trying to remember how many 9s make 72.
- So, you were using the inverse of multiplication model!
- How did we become teachers without knowing this?

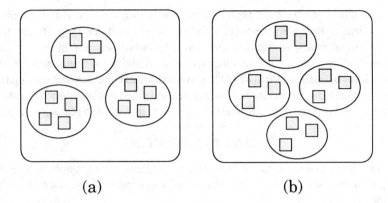

(a)   (b)

Figure 4.4   Two interpretations of '12 ÷ 3': (a) Sharing (b) Inverse of multiplication

In our experience, it seems that teachers of young children tend to emphasize the first model when introducing division to young children, presumably because they perceive 'sharing' as an everyday concept with which children are familiar. There is a tendency therefore for the words 'shared between', 'shared by' or even just 'share' to be attached firmly to the symbol, as though this is what division really means. We must argue, therefore, just as we argued that subtraction is not just 'take away', that division is not just 'sharing'. In exactly the same way that we saw that the take-away model of subtraction was a limited aspect of less long-term significance than, say, the comparison or the inverse of addition models, we must note that the sharing model of division is a limited view and of less significance in the long term than the inverse of multiplication model.

Consider, for example, a division statement like 6 ÷ 0.25. I can happily press the appropriate keys on my calculator and obtain the answer 24, but what might this mean in concrete terms? It certainly could not mean '6 cakes shared between 0.25 of a person makes 24 each'! However, I might want to calculate 6 ÷ 0.25 if I needed to find out how many articles costing twenty-five pence each could be bought for six pounds. So, in this sense, 6 ÷ 0.25 means 'how many 0.25's make 6?' – in other words, it is interpreted using the inverse of multiplication model.

When division is extended into contexts other than just sets of things, such as the money context example given above, both models may be encountered. But the sharing model only makes sense when the second number is a cardinal number, that is a number representing a set of things, normally the number of people receiving a portion or the number of portions being measured out. So we might encounter the sharing model of division in the context of liquid volume if we have 750 ml of wine to share out into five equal portions, or in the context of money if we have £750 to share equally between five people. On the other hand, we would encounter the inverse of multiplication model of division if we needed to find how many 150 ml glasses of wine could be poured from a 750 ml bottle, or how many articles costing £150 each could be bought with £750.

It will help children to connect these two models of division together if once again they are encouraged to associate rectangular arrays with the idea of division. A child could, for example, be given twelve counters and challenged to find different ways of arranging them in a rectangular array. Figure 4.5, showing one such possible arrangement, could then lead to discussion both about how many counters in each of the three rows across the page and also about how many rows of three coming down the page.

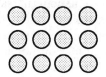

Figure 4.5   One way of arranging twelve counters in an array

The idea of division as the inverse of multiplication leads to two further interpretations. Since one model of multiplication is repeated addition, it follows that a possible model for division is *repeated subtraction*. In this interpretation '12 ÷ 3' might be thought of as 'How many times can I take 3 away from 12 until there is nothing left?' This is clearly very similar to the question 'How many 3s in 12?', so even if we regard it as a different model it seems likely that there will not be much difficulty in learning to connect the same symbols with both questions.

A more-difficult aspect of division arises from the inverse of the scaling model of multiplication. This is the *ratio* model of division. In this model, '12 ÷ 3' might be thought of as meaning something such as 'How many times bigger than 3 is 12?' This is using division to make a *comparison* between two quantities. If, for example, A earns £12 an hour and B earns £3 an hour, then there are in fact two ways of comparing their earnings. We could, on the one hand, use the comparison model of subtraction, as discussed in Chapter 3, and conclude that A earns £9 more than B, or B earns £9 less than A. In this way we would be considering the difference between the two quantities. On the other hand, we could consider the ratio, using this model of division to conclude that A earns four times as much as B.

Which of these two ways of making the comparison should be used will depend on the context, although it is often a matter of subjective judgement. It is interesting to note, for example, that there was a time when teams in the English Football League table with the same number of points were ranked according to goal ratio. So a team with 12 goals for and 6 against would be ranked above a team with 17 goals for and 10 against, since the goal ratio of the first team is 2, whereas that of the second team is only 1.7. Nowadays goal difference is used, so that the two teams would be ranked in the reverse order since a goal difference of 7 is better than a goal difference of 6. Teachers will be familiar with this question as it applies to salary increases. A pay award in which all members receive the same flat-rate increase is seen by some as being fair because it maintains the existing differences in salaries, but is seen by others as being unfair because it does not preserve the existing ratios between salaries. The latter favour a pay award in which all receive the same percentage increase because this preserves the existing ratios. This is a nice example of the way in which some mathematical transformations (the salary increases) preserve some equivalences and destroy others (i.e. the existing salary difference and ratios).

Children's stories for division statements again give us some very interesting insights into their understanding of the operation. Most use the sharing model: 'There was a boy and he had 12 stones so he shared them out into 3 piles. How many stones were there in each pile.' 'There were 12 dollys. If there were 3 girls how many dolls would each girl get?'

But others use the inverse of multiplication model with equal confidence: 'Tom had 12 butterflies and he wanted them in sets of 3. How many sets?' 'On the class outing 12 children were going. The head dived 3 children in each car. How many cars did he need?'

There are, of course, those for whom division is something you do in school without any apparent meaning or purpose other than satisfying the teacher: 'One day in class the teacher asked Ben the answer to 12 shared by 3. Ben didn't know and he got an essay.' Other stories children write for '12 ÷ 3' suggest that we might be deceiving ourselves in suggesting that sharing, in the way intended when doing division in school, is an experience with which children are familiar. Children have many experiences of sharing in their lives, but most of them are nothing like what we expect them to do when we give them '12 ÷ 3'.

For a start, it is most unlikely that a child would share their twelve cakes between their three friends and not have any for themselves. Children normally 'share with', not 'share between'. Parents and teachers share things out between children and seem happy to exclude themselves, but children share with their friends: 'Tim had 12 cakes he shard them out with 3 of his friends.' 'I had 12 mabels and had to share them with 3 freinds.'

Second, sharing equally is a peculiarly mathematical process, not always reflected in the sharing experiences of everyday life: 'The girl had 12 pens and her friend borrowed 3. Her other 2 friends had 1 each. How many did she have left?' Third, children experience sharing when they are told to share their possessions with another person. This can take a number of forms. For example, the child might have twelve items and agree to share three of them. This invalid interpretation of division is no doubt prompted by the unhelpful language pattern, 'twelve share three': 'The boy had 12 sweets and he ate one and gave 2 away to his friends. How many left?' 'I had 12 cars I shared 3 of them.'

Sometimes two children with unequal possessions might agree to share them by a process of pooling their resources: 'One boy had 12 conkers the other had 3 conkers. When they shared the conkers they had equal amounts and they threw the remainder conker away.' So we are suggesting that 'sharing between' is actually a more sophisticated and abstract idea than we might imagine, and also that it is not in the long term the most important model of division.

- I can see that but what do you call the sign?

Of course, in real situations division is sometimes sharing, and when this is the actual concrete situation being attended to then it is appropriate to use this language, although we must take note of the distinction between 'sharing between' and 'sharing with' highlighted above, as well as the other possible interpretations of sharing. Children will need specific help in establishing the pattern of language: 'twelve shared between three is four each'. But again there are two levels of language here, as was the case with subtraction. There is the formal language that goes with the concept, such as 'twelve divided by three' and the language appropriate to the physical situation. This might be 'twelve shared between three', but it might equally well be 'twelve shared into groups of three', depending on what you are actually doing with the counters on the table in front of you.

CONTEXTS

We encounter operations with numbers not just when dealing with sets of things, but also in a variety of measurement contexts. A major part of the development of understanding of the number operations is the establishment of connections between the symbols and language associated with the operation and the various models of the operation as they are met in a variety of real contexts. So, for example, we discuss in Chapter 3 the particularly complex network of connections involved in the comparison model of subtraction as it is encountered in contexts of length, weight, time, and so on.

When we develop a similar scenario for multiplication and division we find that one of the reasons for the greater difficulty involved in understanding these operations is that they often arise in two different contexts simultaneously. We have already hinted at this problem in discussing multiplication earlier in this chapter, when we noted that the two numbers involved in a multiplication statement have to represent different sorts of things. This contrasts with addition and subtraction where the two numbers involved always represent the same sort of thing: we add a set to a set, a price to a price, a length to a length, and so on.

But if we consider possible contexts to be, for example, sets, money, length and distance, weight, liquid volume and capacity, and time, then any two of these might produce a possible real situation in which multiplication and division have some application and meaning.

We will illustrate this first with a number of examples of situations that might correspond to the calculation '9 × 3'. For example, in the contexts of money and weight, we use the repeated addition model of multiplication for finding the cost of three pounds of potatoes at nine pence a pound. In the contexts of time and distance we might be calculating how far we can go in three hours if we cycle at nine miles per hour. In the contexts of money and liquid volume we might be calculating the cost of nine litres of wine at three pounds per litre.

Second, we might consider some examples of pairs of contexts in which '12 ÷ 3' might have an application and meaning. The contexts of weight and money, for example, might give rise to an application of division when finding the equivalent price per kilogram of a three-kilogram pack of some material that costs twelve pounds. The contexts of distance and time involve division when calculating average speed: 'What is my average speed if I walk twelve miles in three hours?' And the contexts of money and time produce problems such as calculating your rate of pay if you have earned twelve pounds in three hours.

The conclusion we come to, then, is that understanding of multiplication and division once again involves the building up of a complex network of connections between the symbols, the language, both formal and informal, the pictures associated with the operations, particularly rectangular arrays, and the surprising variety of concrete situations, contexts and combinations of contexts in which they arise. We leave the last word on this subject to two of our story-writers: 'Once there was a boy at school and he was given some sums to do but when he got to number five he could not do it. The sum was 9 × 3.' '12 ÷ 3 = 4 and the King of Scotland did not know what it ment.' Not just the King of Scotland, presumably.

SUMMARY OF KEY IDEAS IN CHAPTER 4

1. One category of situations to which the language and symbols of multiplication can be connected is repeated addition. This model is most clearly seen in the context of sets, but extends naturally to measuring contexts.
2. Multiplication is commutative: in other words, for any two numbers, a and b, $a \times b = b \times a$.
3. The commutative property of multiplication is most clearly seen in rectangular arrays.
4. Strictly speaking, in the repeated addition model '9 × 3' means '3 sets of 9'. But once commutativity is established it can be taken to mean either '3 sets of 9' or '9 sets of 3'.

5. Another category of situations to which the language and symbols of multiplication can be connected is scaling.
6. Four categories of situations to which the language and symbols of division can be connected are sharing (between), the inverse of multiplication, repeated subtraction and ratio.
7. Ratio and difference are two ways of comparing quantities, using division and subtraction respectively.
8. Children have many other experiences of sharing that do not correspond to the sharing-between model of division.
9. Multiplication and division often arise in situations involving two different contexts, such as money and weight, or distance and time.

SOME ACTIVITIES WITH CHILDREN

Activity 4.1: stories (multiplication and division)

Objective To help children connect the symbols for multiplication and division with a wide range of situations and language.

Method Give children some multiplication and division statements (e.g. 8×3, $15 \div 5$) and get them to write stories to go with them. This is handled in the same way as Activity 3.1. Encourage children to use the different models and contexts for multiplication and division, by giving the beginnings of some stories. For example, children could be asked to write a story for '8×3' beginning 'Choc bars are 8p each ...'; or a story for '$15 \div 5$' beginning 'Mary had £15 to spend on records. If a record costs ...'.

Another approach is to specify contexts, for example, by asking children to write a story for '8×3' that is about a farmer who sells potatoes at 8p a pound; or a story about '$15 \div 5$' that is about a person who walks for 15 miles.

Activity 4.2: swaps (multiplication and division)

Objective To develop connections between language, symbols, concrete experience and pictures, for the concepts of multiplication and division.

Materials and method The same as Activity 3.2, except using stories with multiplication and division examples. For example, a possible starting point might be the story, 'How many £16 chairs can my Mum buy with £80?'; then this could be swapped for coins, calculator, symbols and a number-line drawing.

Activity 4.3: sentences (multiplication and division)

Objective To develop language patterns for multiplication and division.

Materials Several sets of strips of card with the following words or phrases written on them – divided by, multiplied by, times, shared, between, makes, is, equals, sets of, altogether, each – and several sets of cards with appropriate numerals and signs written on them; counting materials and a number line.

Method As in Activity 3.3, a small group of children is given three numbers and challenged to use the cards to make up as many different sentences as they can using these three numbers. Figure 4.6 shows some examples of what might be achieved with the numbers 3, 4 and 12.

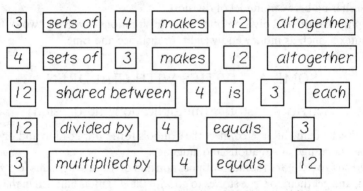

Figure 4.6   Sentences for 3, 4 and 12 (Activity 4.3)

Activity 4.4: number-line multiplication

Objective To provide experience of multiplication in the context of a number line.

Materials Two conventional dice numbered from 1 to 6; a counter (or an appropriate small toy); a number line marked from 0 to 36; two small flags of some sort (for a more advanced game, use dodecahedra dice with faces numbered from 1 to 12, and a number line marked from 0 to 144).

Method This is a multiplication version of Activity 3.4, for a small group of players. The player going first places the flags on the number line on any two numbers of their choosing. Each then plays in turn as follows. They place the counter on the zero mark and throw the two dice. One score represents the step size and the other the number of steps. So a score of 3 and 5, for example, might be '3 steps of 5' or '5 steps of 3'. (Children can discover for themselves the principle of commutativity in this context.) Once again they have to predict where they will land, and score a point if they are correct. If they finish on a number with a flag on it they receive a bonus point. The positioning of the flags causes some interesting discussions – for example, 12 is a better bet than 13 if you are looking for bonus points!

Activity 4.5: what did I do? (36, +, −, ×, ÷ version)

Objective To give children experience of addition and subtraction, and multiplication and division, as inverse operations.

Materials One calculator per two children; plastic pennies as prizes.

Method This is an extension of Activity 3.5 using all four operations. Players take it in turns to challenge each other with the question, 'What did I do?' The number 36 is entered on the calculator. Player A presses one operation key (+, −, ×, ÷) followed by a single digit and the equals key. The calculator is then shown to player B who has to (1) state which keys A pressed and (2) press one operation key followed by a single digit and the equals key, in order to get the 36 back on display. B wins one penny for correctly stating which keys A pressed, and a further penny for getting back to 36. It is then player B's turn to challenge A.

Interesting discussions will arise in three particular cases:

1. When the first player has performed an operation that leaves 36 on display, since this could be achieved in four different ways!
2. If a player attempts to divide by zero.
3. When the first player divides by 7, the second player multiplies by 7 and then finds that instead of 36 the calculator displays 35.999999.

Activity 4.6: arrays

Objective To connect multiplication and division with the picture of a rectangular array.

Materials Counters or cubes; a calculator.

Method First, as suggested earlier in this chapter, the children are sent to explore the environment in search of examples of rectangular arrays, recording their findings as shown in Figure 4.3. A calculator can be used to associate the array with the symbol for multiplication, and to check the total number of objects in the array.

Then, back in the classroom − after discussing and sharing their example of arrays with the teacher − children in small groups are given a pile of counters or cubes to use in a simple investigation. The challenge is to find out which numbers can be made into rectangular arrays and which ones cannot. For example, 7 cannot, but 12 can be done in four different ways (3 rows of 4, 4 rows of 3, 2 rows of 6, 6 rows of 2).

Note A single line of objects does not count as an array.

Activity 4.7: I have, who has? (addition and subtraction stories)

Objective To practise using all the models and language for multiplication and division.

Materials Prepare a set of 16 cards with 'questions' on one side and the corresponding 'answers' on the other side, using the same cyclic scheme as explained in Activity 2.2 and Activity 3.7, with the question on one card answered on the reverse side of the next.

This time use as questions a series of statements or stories covering the whole range of models and language for multiplication and division. Here are some suggestions, with the corresponding answers in brackets after each one:

1. Four times three. (4 × 3)
2. How much for 4 apples at 5p each? (5 × 4)
3. Debbie shared 12p between 4 people. How much each? (12 ÷ 4)
4. How many 3s in 12? (12 ÷ 3)
5. 20 divided by 4. (20 ÷ 4)
6. 20 multiplied by 4. (20 × 4)
7. John has 4 sets of 12 stamps. How many altogether? (12 × 4)
8. How many times longer than 3 cm is 15 cm? (15 ÷ 3)
9. How many times can 5p be taken away from 15p until there's nothing left? (15 ÷ 5)
10. 4 rows of 15 seats. (15 × 4)
11. John is 12 years old. His Mum is 3 times as old as him. How old is she? (12 × 3)
12. How many 5p's make 20p? (20 ÷ 5)
13. 20 add 20 add 20. (20 × 3)
14. Three fives. (5 × 3)
15. Half of 20. (20 ÷ 2)
16. Two people shared 12 sweets. How many each? (12 ÷ 2)

Method As in Activities 2.2 and 3.7.

SUGGESTIONS FOR FURTHER READING

Anghileri, J. (1985) 'Should we say times?' *Mathematics in Schools*, Vol. 14, no.3, pp. 24–6. (This article considers the meaning of multiplication and methods of teaching it to avoid later confusion.)

Davies, J. (1988) 'From foxes to Ferraris', *Junior Education*, March, pp. 20–1. (In this short article, Davies describes a highly-successful investigational project involving a new by-pass, some enthusiastic juniors, multiplication, division and much calculator practice!)

Desforges, A. and Desforges, C. (1980) 'Number-based strategies of sharing in young children', *Educational Studies*, Vol. 6, pp. 97–109. (A rare account full of insights into pre-schoolers' understanding of the concept of sharing.)

Dickson, L., Brown, M. and Gibson, O. (1984) *Children Learning Mathematics*, Cassell Education for the Schools Council, London, pp. 231–8. (In these few pages the authors consider the problems children experience with multiplication and division and the pedagogical implications.)

Newman, C. (1985) 'How children divide', *Mathematics Teaching*, Vol. 112, pp. 18–19. (Newman describes how her class of 10-year-olds solved division problems. She concludes that it is essential that teachers talk to pupils individually about their work in order to learn something of their mathematical thinking.)

5
MEASUREMENT

In earlier chapters we have frequently found ourselves discussing operations with numbers in various measuring contexts. We will now, therefore, turn our attention to the mathematical ideas involved in measurement itself.

WHAT DO WE MEASURE?

Some of the comments that emerged when we raised this question with teachers set the agenda for the first part of our discussion of measurement:

- Length seems to be the most straightforward form of measurement, because the children can see what they're measuring.
- It's not quite the same when you're measuring the distance from one point to another. That's much more abstract, isn't it?
- My children do a lot with volume and capacity. But we normally only deal with measuring out stuff like water and sand, and pouring it into various containers.
- I'm never sure whether we're talking about the size of the container or the amount of water in it.
- What about mass and weight?
- Aren't they the same thing? Some books say you should talk about the mass and some say weight.
- That always confuses me, so I just ignore it and talk about weight.
- We measure time as well, but children find that very difficult.
- I think that's because you can't actually see what you're measuring.

Inevitably, we tend to think of measurement as being about the things that we measure, such as length, volume, weight, time and so on, rather than considering it in terms of the principles that underlie all measuring experiences. Of course, length, weight, and so on, are all very important concepts. But we might note that some of the basic principles of measurement can be experienced by children through invented measuring scales for such things as how much they enjoyed various television programmes or what sort of a day it's been. Their enjoyment could be measured, for example, using a system of star ratings, four stars for a great programme, three for a quite good programme, and so on. This experience, although subjective, contains the essential elements of comparison, ordering and transitivity that lie at the heart of measurement. These and other basic principles of measurement are considered later in this chapter.

But most of the time in primary schools, children's experiences of measuring will focus on length and distance, volume and capacity, time of day and time intervals, and mass and weight. Some comments about possible confusions involved in these concepts should be made.

LENGTH AND DISTANCE

To demonstrate that understanding of the concept of length is not as straightforward as might at first appear, consider some of the different types of situations to which, for example, the group of symbols '90 cm' might be connected. First we might connect it to a straight part of some solid object, such as the edge of a table, and conclude that the table is 90 cm long, or 90 cm wide. Then we might connect it with a straight line drawn on the floor, on the board, on a piece of paper. We sometimes connect it to an imaginary straight line running through an irregular object, such as a child, for example, when finding that the height of the child is 90 cm. We could also connect it to an imaginary straight line passing through the air, in order to talk about the height of a table. In the last two examples, the convention is that the imaginary line must be vertical. In other circumstances, such as finding the gap between two cupboards, the convention requires a horizontal line at right angles to the edges of the cupboards.

Again we might connect it to an imaginary straight line joining two points or objects, when we say that they are 90 cm apart, or when we talk about the distance from one point to the other. We may have to imagine a piece of string stretched between the two points. Then we might connect it to other than straight lines on various objects, for example, when measuring someone's waist as 90 cm. And then we might also connect it to other than straight paths, for example, when we add up the lengths of the four sides of a rectangle to find that the perimeter is 90 cm, or when we find the length of a curved path from A to B to be 90 cm.

This analysis helps us to understand some of the confusions that arise in children's minds because once again we connect the same symbols to such a variety of situations. In Figure 5.1, for example, the question might be posed as

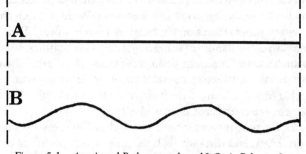

Figure 5.1   Are A and B the same length? Or is B longer?

to whether A is longer than, shorter than or the same length as B. In one sense it is true to say that A and B are the same length, if we think of B as an object and the length of it as the imaginary horizontal line passing through it. But in another sense it is true to say that B is longer than A, if we focus on the lengths of the paths.

VOLUME AND CAPACITY

These two words sometimes cause a little confusion, not just because the word 'volume' is mostly associated nowadays with a control on a television set. The volume of something is the amount of three-dimensional space it occupies. Volume is normally measured in cubic units, such as cubic centimetres and cubic feet. So we might say, for example, that the volume of a cuboid 3 cm long, 2 cm wide and 4 cm high is 24 cubic centimetres, meaning that it occupies the same amount of space as 24 centimetre cubes.

Only containers have capacity. The capacity of a container is simply the volume of liquid it will hold. Although capacity and liquid volume could be measured in the same units as volume in general, special units have developed that are often used for measuring these aspects in particular, such as litres and pints.

TIME AND TIME AGAIN

There are in fact two very different concepts associated with time, which children may measure. First there is 'the time' at which something occurs. We use time in this sense when we consult our watch to find the time of day, or make an appointment for a particular day of the month, or recall the year in which something took place.

There is next 'the time' that something takes to happen or the time that passes between two events. This is the notion of a time interval, which we might measure in seconds, minutes, hours, days, weeks, months, years, decades or centuries. Age, being the time interval from birth to the present, is one example of this rather abstract concept that children handle with surprising confidence. No doubt this is related to the fact that their age is very much part of their identity: the first two questions anyone asks a child are 'What's your name?' and 'How old are you?'

Teachers of young children should note that 'time of day' and 'time interval' are two very different concepts. We shall see later in this chapter that they also have different mathematical properties.

MASS AND WEIGHT

This is a tricky one, which we approach with some hesitation. There is an important distinction in scientific terms between the mass and the weight of an object. Strictly speaking, units such as grams, kilograms, pounds and ounces are units of mass, not units of weight. We will, therefore, refer to those sets of plastic shapes or pieces of metal that we use for weighing things as, for example, ten-gram masses, kilogram masses, four-ounce masses, and so on. If an object balances against a kilogram mass, as shown in Figure 5.2, then we deduce that it is also a kilogram mass. The mass of an object is a measure of the amount of stuff making up the object, the quantity of matter in it, which is something to do with the number of atoms involved. This is not the same thing as the volume, because in some objects the matter is more densely compressed together than in others.

However, when you hold an object in your hand you cannot actually experience its mass. You cannot perceive it, count it, smell it, feel it. It is the weight, not the mass, that you can feel and to which your muscles respond. This weight is the gravitational force pulling the object down towards the ground. Since weight is a force, it should be measured in the units used for measuring force. In the metric system, force – and therefore weight – is measured in newtons. Without being too technical, it may help the reader to know that a newton is about the weight of a small apple. On the earth's surface a mass of one

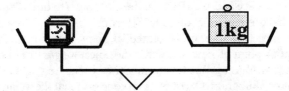

Figure 5.2   An object weighing the same as a kilogram mass

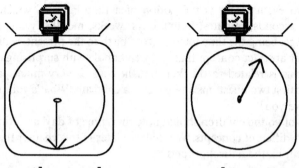

on the earth   on the moon

Figure 5.3   Change in weight indicated on spring-type weighing scales

kilogram has a weight of nearly 10 newtons (more precisely, g newtons, where g is the acceleration due to gravity).

Having seen film of astronauts on the moon, we are all familiar with the idea that if we were to take the object concerned to the moon, where the gravitational force would be smaller, the weight of the object would be reduced. Our one-kilogram mass would now weigh only about one and a half newtons. This is actually because the mass of the moon is much smaller than the mass of the earth, and therefore the gravitational pull is weaker.

This change in weight would show up if we were weighing our object on a spring-type weighing device, as shown in Figure 5.3. But it is interesting to observe that the situation in Figure 5.2 would not change if we took the balances to the moon. It appears therefore that the two weighing devices are measuring different things!

The balance-type weighing device enables us to deduce the mass of an object, by balancing it against an equal mass. The spring-type weighing device clearly responds to weight. The former would give you the same result wherever you used it. The latter would give slightly different readings at the bottom of a coal mine or at the top of Mount Everest, and a significantly different reading on the moon. In practice, of course, we will not often take our kitchen or bathroom scales to the moon. So the scales can safely be graduated in grams and kilograms, or pounds and ounces, and you can be confident that when you weigh something on the earth's surface and the arrow on the dial points to one kilogram then you do actually have a mass of about one kilogram.

Teachers may, therefore, be perplexed to know that it is actually incorrect from a scientific point of view to say that the object *weighs* one kilogram or that the *weight* of the object is one kilogram. Strictly speaking, it is the *mass* of the object that is one kilogram. Of course, everyone says that the weight of the object is one kilogram, and the idea of measuring weight in newtons is too sophisticated for primary-school children. But, later on, many of these children will need, in their physics lessons, to distinguish between weight and mass, and the majority will find this very difficult. No doubt part of the difficulty will be unlearning the erroneous language of primary school and the market-place.

We offer below some suggestions that might help with this problem. These are scientifically correct, mathematically sound and reasonably straightforward, but we accept the fact that the reader may choose to ignore them! First, we refer to those things we use for weighing as masses, not weights. The word 'mass' is thus encountered when we shift from weighing with non-standard units to weighing with standard units. In the classroom cupboard we will have boxes of one-gram masses, ten-gram masses, hundred-gram masses, and so on.

Young children's experience of weighing should be with balance-type weighing devices. When we have weighed something we say something along the lines of 'The book weighs the same as twenty marbles' or 'The book weighs the same as a mass of two hundred grams' or, simply, 'The book weighs the same as two hundred grams'. The key phrase is 'weighs the same as', emphasizing the equivalence that has emerged. If an object weighs the same as, say, a mass of two hundred grams then we can also say that this object has a mass of two hundred grams.

MEASUREMENT IN GENERAL

In this section we will consider what might be some of the fundamental mathematical ideas involved in the process of measuring. These ideas include the notion of comparison and ordering, the principles of transitivity and conservation, and the idea of a unit.

We are concerned first, then, with the mathematical ideas common to most aspects of measurement. However, there are actually different types of measuring scales, with different mathematical properties, and these are considered towards the end of the chapter.

Comparison

The primary purpose of making a measurement is to make comparisons between two items according to the magnitude of some attribute, such as length, weight, capacity, age, value, and so on, and thereby to put them in order. Associated with this idea is the extensive set of language of comparison discussed in Chapter 3: longer, shorter, heavier, lighter, younger, older, and so on.

We should note that, particularly in the early stages of measuring some attributes, comparisons of this sort can often be made directly without the use of any measuring units. So two children can stand next to each other and determine who is the taller and who is the shorter. Two objects can be put on either end of a simple see-saw balance and a deduction made about which is the heavier and which is the lighter. It is important at this stage of the child's development of understanding of the particular measuring concept that they experience objects that exaggerate the attribute in question. A large, light object can be balanced against a small, heavy object in order to focus the attention on the weight rather than the size. Water can be poured from a tall jar with a small capacity into a short, squat jar with a large capacity. Comparing by weight pairs of identical-looking sealed yoghurt cartons filled with materials of different density – sand, sawdust, ball-bearings – again focuses the attention on the one way in which they are different, namely in terms of their heaviness.

We should remind ourselves of the fundamental idea that every comparison statement has an alternative equivalent form, and that children should be encouraged always to make both statements. This is such a key aspect of language and mathematical development that it cannot be overemphasized. In purely mathematical terms, we are interpreting in measuring contexts one of the basic properties of an ordering relationship, namely

$$\text{`}a > b\text{'} \text{ is equivalent to `}b < a\text{'.}$$

Here are some examples of what we have in mind, which demonstrate that this is a key principle that pervades all areas of measurement:

- The table is higher than the desk.
  The desk is lower than the table.
- Breakfast is earlier than dinner.
  Dinner is later than breakfast.
- The book is heavier than the pencil.
  The pencil is lighter than the book.
- John is older than Mary.
  Mary is younger than John.
- London is bigger than Norwich.
  Norwich is smaller than London.
- A motorway is wider than my street.
  My street is narrower than a motorway.
- My car is faster than your car.
  Your car is slower than my car.

In making comparisons of this sort we are attending to what is different about two objects, in other words, to a transformation that occurs when we shift our attention from some attribute of one to the same attribute of the other, such as height, weight, and so on. As in the example of the identical yoghurt cartons, the two objects may in all other respects be the same.

But there is, of course, another possibility when two objects are compared for some particular attribute: we may decide that they are equal. So two objects, such as a book and a box, may be very different in a number of respects, such as their size or their shape, but be equivalent in another. For example, they may weigh the same. So we see that what have been referred to in Chapter 1 as the concepts of transformation and equivalence are here associated with the most fundamental idea of measuring. These two ideas appear to permeate all mathematical thinking. The equivalence notion, 'is the same as', will turn up frequently in measuring experiences, in such language forms as 'is the same length as', 'weighs the same as', 'happens at the same time as', and so on.

Ordering and transitivity

A second important principle common to any ordering relationship is that of *transitivity*. This principle is evident when three or more objects are being ordered according to a particular attribute, such as their lengths, their weights, their time of day, their capacity, and so on. In Figure 5.4 (a) the arrow could represent any one of our comparison statements, such as 'is longer than', 'is lighter than', 'is earlier than', 'holds more than', and so on. The objects A, B and C have been ordered using such a relationship, by comparing A with B and then B with C. The principle of transitivity allows us to make the logical deduction about the relationship between A and C, shown in Figure 5.4(b), i.e. A is longer than C, or A is lighter than C, and so on. The relation is said to be transitive when the following is necessarily the case: if it occurs between A and B and between B and C, then it can be 'carried across' directly from A to C.

Formally, this principle is expressed as follows:

$$\text{if } A > B \text{ and } B > C \text{ then } A > C$$

or

$$\text{if } A < B \text{ and } B < C \text{ then } A < C.$$

All measuring relationships satisfy this property: putting things in order is a fundamental property of any form of measurement.

Clearly, the arrows in Figure 5.4 could also represent equivalence, for example, 'is the same length as', 'weighs the same as', and so on. We should note, therefore, that equivalence also satisfies transitivity:

$$\text{if } A = B \text{ and } B = C \text{ then } A = C.$$

Although this might appear to be a rather obvious statement, in the context of measurement it is actually very significant, since it is this property that allows us to make repeated copies of standard measurements, such as the kilogram or the

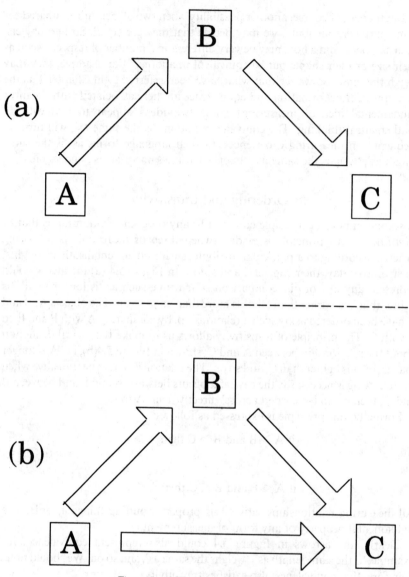

Figure 5.4   The principle of transitivity

metre, without always going back to the originals!

To understand the concept of transitivity it might be helpful for the reader to experience some non-exemplars as well as exemplars. We have seen how the arrows in Figure 5.4 might represent any relationship of the form 'is greater than', 'is less than' or 'is the same as'. But not all mathematical relationships are transitive. In fact, part of our understanding of any relationship must be an implicit awareness of whether it is or is not transitive. To demonstrate this the reader may care to assess their understanding of the concept of 'factor' by asking this question: if the arrows on Figure 5.4(a) represent 'is a factor of', where A, B and C are three integers, does the relationship between A and C shown in Figure 5.4(b) necessarily follow?

- What's a factor?
- A number that divides exactly into another number. For example, four is a factor of twelve, because four divides into twelve exactly.
- So, if A is a factor of B and B is a factor of C we want to know if A is a factor of C.
- I haven't the foggiest idea. It might be, I suppose.
- Four is a factor of twelve and twelve is a factor of 24. That works. Four is a factor of 24.
- Will it always work?

Try the same exercise with other mathematical relationships, such as 'is one more than', 'is half of', 'is a multiple of'. The facility with which you make the deduction about whether or not A related to B and B related to C necessarily implies that A is related to C is a good indicator of your understanding of the mathematical relationship. If you do not find it immediately obvious then you are in exactly the same situation as young children learning about measurement. Having compared A with B and B with C they will not automatically make the deduction about the relationship between A and C.

Therefore, since transitivity is such a fundamental property of measurement, then it is self-evident that children should have many experiences of putting three (or more) objects in order according to their length, their weight, their capacity, and so on. It would appear likely that through experience of this kind of ordering activity they will be helped to achieve this mathematical structure in their thinking about measurement in general.

Conservation

Another fundamental principle that applies to many aspects of measurement is that known as *conservation*. This refers, for example, to the fact that a ball of Plasticene will still weigh the same when it has been squashed into a sausage shape or broken up into a number of smaller pieces; that a piece of carpet still covers the same amount of floor when it is moved to a different part of the room or cut into two smaller pieces and rearranged; that the volume of water in a tall, thin flask does not change when it is poured into a short, squat flask; that the

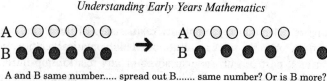

A and B same number..... spread out B....... same number? Or is B more?

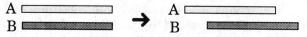

A and B same volume...... pour B into new container..... same volume?

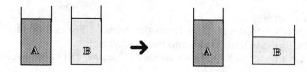

A and B same length..... displace B....... same length? Or is B longer?

Figure 5.5 Assessing understanding of conservation

length of a pencil remains the same when it is displaced a little to the right. Figure 5.5 provides some examples of tasks that have sometimes been used to assess children's grasp of this principle in various measuring contexts.

Demonstrating a grasp of this principle of conservation, first of all with number, then with length, weight, area and volume has been identified by Piaget as one of the key indicators of a child's intellectual development. However, many of the tasks used to assess the child's grasp of conservation, such as those in Figure 5.5, have been justifiably criticized as not being embedded in a context that has any meaning or purpose for a child. It appears to us to be the case that quite young children seem to use the principle of conservation of measurement quite happily when engaged in a purposeful task in a meaningful context. When, for example, they are doing cooking, they will measure out quantities of water and flour, and then proceed to transfer these from one container to another without any apparent concern that these activities might alter the quantities they measured out in the first place!

In spite of such reservations as these about some of the methods used to assess children's understanding of conservation, we should stress that this is nevertheless an important component of measurement, and children will certainly benefit from activities and discussion designed to focus their attention upon this principle. In fact, it provides us with yet another experience of our concepts of transformation and equivalence. What the child has to grasp, for example, is that if you take a quantity of water in a container and apply to it certain transformations, such as pouring it into a different-shaped container, then the volume of water is the same. In other words, there is an equivalence, something the same about the two situations, in spite of the transformation that has occurred to, say, the height of the water level or the shape of the water. In fact, we could say that what the child has to learn is which transformations preserve which equivalences and which transformations destroy which equivalences. If you take a square piece of paper and transform it by moving it to a different position or by cutting it up into two triangles, then the area is preserved: it will still cover the same amount of the table surface. If, on the other hand, you screw the paper up into a tight, little ball, or set light to it, then these are transformations that destroy this equivalence. The reader will find it a useful exercise to analyse, in terms of which equivalences are preserved or destroyed, transformations such as re-arranging a few building blocks, boiling some water, sharpening a pencil, rolling up a tape-measure, taking an object to the moon or putting the clocks forward for summer time.

Units

Common to all aspects of measurement is the idea of a *unit*. Instead of just using measurement concepts to order two or more objects, we now move to comparing some attribute of a single object with a number of equal units. So a child would move on from making statements such as 'The book is longer than the pencil' to statements such as 'The table is about ten pencils long.'

- What about arbitrary units? I'm very uncertain about the value of children using arbitrary units for measuring.

It is conventional to introduce children to the idea of a unit through the use of *non-standard* (sometimes called arbitrary) units, as in the example of measuring the length of a desk in pencils, or weighing objects with marbles, before moving on to standard units such as centimetres and grams. A number of reasons are put forward for the value of this experience.

First, children are introduced to the concept of measuring in units through familiar objects, such as pencils, marbles, hand spans, feet, and so on, rather than going straight into these mysterious things called centimetres and grams. In this way they are not required to handle a new piece of vocabulary for the unit at the same time as meeting a new measuring experience. Certainly as far as the mathematical ideas involved are concerned, there is no difference between measuring a table in pencils and measuring it in centimetres, so if children find a familiar non-standard unit less threatening all well and good.

Second, it is suggested that the non-standard unit can be a more appropriate size of unit for the first practical measuring tasks that young children will undertake. Centimetres may be too small and therefore too numerous for your first experience of measuring the length of the desk top, or the height of a friend, and metres are clearly too large a unit for this purpose. Grams are very small units for weighing most of the objects around the classroom, such as books, scissors, shoes, and so on, and a kilogram will put the child in hospital if dropped on their foot. Something like a marble is likely to be much more appropriate and will result in measurements of just a handful of units, rather than hundreds of them to begin with.

Third, the experience can open children to the idea that scales can be invented for a particular measuring task when a standard scale is not available, or when the standard scale is inappropriate. For example, one group of children invented their own scale for measuring the dirtiness of water after washing clothes in it.

Fourth, we can note that adults do not always use standard units. Whether or not they do might depend on the accuracy required by the task. For example, most of us are happy to measure out fertilizer for our lawns by the handful, and will often use spans and paces for certain stages of practical jobs in the home.

Finally, it is argued that through using non-standard units children will become aware of the need for a standard unit when, for example, they discover that the classroom is twenty paces wide when they measure it, but only eleven paces wide when the teacher measures it.

- When my 6-year-olds were measuring lengths in spans and feet they made me do them all as well. They seemed fascinated by the idea that my span or my feet always gave a smaller number.
- They do seem to pick up this idea of the need for a standard unit quite quickly.
- Quite often they've met the standard units from shopping anyway.

One infant teacher had serious doubts about using units like spans and paces with young children:

I always find an element of competition creeps in when they start measuring in hand spans or paces, and the maths goes out of the window. One girl refused to admit that her span was shorter than someone else's and got quite upset. Then when they were pacing out the length of the corridor all the boys started taking enormous leaps, rather than strides, to see who could do it in the smallest number!

We take this teacher's point, and it may be that there are occasions when impersonal spoons and sticks might be preferable as units to individuals' spans and strides. But we wonder whether it is really the case that the maths has gone out of the window in these examples. These children seem very aware of the significance of the size of the units being used.

Metric and Imperial units

The ability to make reasonable *estimates* of quantities in various units is an important component of our understanding of the concepts of measurement. For example, our own grasp of some of the standard units used for measurement may be indicated by how easily we answer questions such as these:

- What is your approximate height in centimetres?
- If you stood on the bathroom scales roughly how many kilograms would be indicated?
- What is the approximate temperature today in degrees celsius?
- What is a standard spoonful of medicine in millilitres?
- Roughly how far is it in kilometres from where you live to the centre of London?
- About how many litres of petrol does the tank of your car take?
- How many cheese sandwiches could you make with one hundred grams of cheese?

This discussion about estimation inevitably raises questions about metric and Imperial units.

- I can do it in feet and inches, or pounds and ounces, but I find it hard in metres or grams.
- The children grow up using metric at school then they can't cope when they come across yards and feet.
- Or pounds and ounces. Shops still sell a lot of things in ounces.
- But isn't everything gradually being changed to metric?

In the UK we find ourselves today in a rather unsatisfactory position regarding the use of metric and Imperial units. The situation in the USA is similar, with both systems living side by side and only slow progress towards metrication. These situations contrast with a number of other English-speaking countries, such as Australia, New Zealand and Canada, who have made a much more wholehearted national commitment to the conversion to metric units.

In 1965 the British government acceded to industry's request for the UK to adopt metric units, and we were soon led to believe that, under the guidance of the Metrication Board, by the late 1970s everything would have changed from the old Imperial units to the universally-accepted metric units. Primary-school mathematics schemes were changed to prepare the next generation of children for the new metric world in which they would grow up. Primary-school teachers were suddenly given new freedom in mathematics lessons as they were able to ditch the teaching of calculations with inches, feet, yards and miles, or with ounces, pounds, stones, hundredweights and tons. Now everything would be based on tens, hundreds and thousands, place value would be reinforced through measuring experiences, and once we all got used to the new units measurement would be so much more rational and straightforward.

Many changes have taken place, of course, such as in the pharmaceutical industry where presumably we are now all accustomed to our plastic spoonfuls of five-millilitre doses from our 200-millilitre bottles of medicine. But many areas of British life have proved to be very resistant to change. Moreover, the decimalization of money in the early 1970s had proved to be an unpopular measure, coinciding with a period of high inflation, with rising prices attributed by many people to the new money. A succession of governments with small majorities did not appear to have the will to push through further unpopular changes to the British way of life. So many Imperial units have survived in many areas of life. And we now have a generation of schoolchildren who have not been taught at school how to deal with them. Furthermore, since the Metrication Board has now been abolished, there is apparently no body with responsibility for overseeing the completion of the task begun in 1965. It may be that more extensive use of metric units may be forced upon us by the closer economic, industrial and commercial ties with Europe, which will come about in 1992. But it seems highly likely that road signs in miles, speeds in miles per hour and pints of beer, for example, will still be with us at the end of the century. And we will no doubt have to continue to cope with the unsatisfactory mixture of units that is evident all around.

- I bought some wood the other day. Its cross-sectional dimensions were in millimetres but it was sold by the foot.
- Sometimes they sell carpet by the square yard and sometimes by the square metre.
- They advertise the price by the square yard because it looks cheaper, but they measure it out by the metre.
- There's a sign on a road near my house which says 'Six foot six inches width restriction, 200 yards ahead'. I looked up in the manual to find out how wide my car was, and it said 1,650 millimetres!
- My brother had to do an exam for a job in the railway and it was all in Imperial units. He couldn't do any of it because he'd been taught metric at school.

If we are preparing our children for the demands of the real world, it means, therefore, that we will have to bring back into their measuring experience at school at an appropriate stage opportunities to measure with all the different units actually used in the world outside. Otherwise we will simply reinforce the idea that what goes on at school has nothing to do with life outside.

SI base units and other metric units

Teachers may come across references to the SI (International System) version of metric units. This is an internationally-accepted convention used in trade and industry, and in technological and scientific work. The main feature of this system is that each aspect of measurement should have just one base unit. Some of these are shown in Table 5.1 for some aspects of measurement likely to concern teachers, together with the appropriate symbol. It is an accident of history that the base unit for mass is the kilogram (kg) not the gram (g).

Table 5.1   Some SI units

Measure	SI unit	Symbol
Length	metre	m
Mass	kilogram	kg
Time	second	s
Area	square metre	m^2
Volume	cubic metre	m^3
Speed	metres per second	m/s

According to the SI convention, all lengths, for example, would be measured in metres. This would mean that the width of a piece of A4 paper should be given as about 0.21 m. If other units are to be used, by the use of various prefixes, then there is a further convention that as far as possible only those representing powers of a thousand should be employed. Some of these are shown in Table 5.2.

Table 5.2   Preferred prefixes

Prefix	Meaning	Symbol	Example
mega	one million	M	1Mg = one million grams
kilo	one thousand	k	1kg = one thousand grams
milli	one thousandth	m	1mm = one thousandth of a metre
micro	one millionth	μ	1μm = one millionth of a metre

The width of the piece of A4 paper could then be given as about 210 mm. However, for practical purposes, other prefixes are required because, for example, in measuring length for many tasks the millimetre is too small and the metre too large. We might find it easier, for example, to give the width of a piece of A4 paper as 21 cm. Some of these other prefixes are shown in Table 5.3.

There are other metric units derived from SI units. The commonest of these is the litre (1) and the associated millilitre (ml), centilitre (cl) and decilitre (dl). We have noticed that bottles of wine are variously labelled as 0.75 litre, 7.5 dl, 75 cl and 750 ml. A litre is the equivalent in liquid volume or capacity of one thousand cubic centimetres. Those who purchase solid fuel, for example, may also

Table 5.3 Some other prefixes

Prefix	Meaning	Symbol	Example
centi	one hundredth	c	1cm = one hundredth of a metre
deci	one tenth	d	1dm = one tenth of a metre
hecto	one hundred	h	1hg = one hundred grams

encounter the tonne, referred to in speech as 'the metric tonne'. This is a thousand kilograms (1,000 kg) or a million grams (i.e. 1 Mg).

We conclude this section with an assortment of facts and conventions about metric units that may be helpful.

- One litre is the same volume as 1,000 cm^3.
- 1 ml is the same volume as 1 cm^3.
- A medicine spoon holds 5 ml.
- Base-ten materials for number work are often based on centimetres.
- If the unit is a centimetre cube then the 'ten' is a decimetre long.
- The 'hundred' is a decimetre square.
- The 'thousand' is a decimetre cube.
- A decimetre cube is 1,000 cm^3, i.e. the same as a litre!
- A litre of water has a mass of 1 kg.
- Hence 1 ml of water has a mass of 1 g.
- And a cubic metre of water has a mass of one tonne (i.e. 1,000 kg).
- The distance from the North Pole to the Equator is approximately ten thousand kilometres.
- A simple pendulum of length 1 m ticks once approximately every second.
- The symbol for litre is l, but avoid this since it is confused with 1 (i.e. one).
- Note the correct spelling of 'gram'.
- The symbol for gram is not gm but g.
- Symbols for units do not have plural forms, so do not write, for example, 5 cms, but 5 cm.
- The symbol for kilo is a lower case k, not a capital K.
- No full stops should be used after a symbol for a unit, such as 5 cm or 10 kg, except at the end of a sentence.

Finally, readers may be reassured that there are no plans to enforce the metrication of time. This may be due to the fact that no one can persuade the earth to orbit the sun in anything other than just over 365 days, and that a seven-day week is apparently ordained by God.

APPROXIMATION AND ACCURACY

An interesting feature of measurement is that nearly all measurement is *approximate*. Except when the measurement is simply a form of counting, such as when 'measuring' the value of the coins in your pocket, we always measure to the nearest something. It is not possible, for example, to make an exact measurement of the length of anything.

● Are you saying that there is not a precise measurement for that table?

That's precisely what we are saying. All we can do is to measure the length of the table to the nearest centimetre, or nearest millimetre, and so on. Even with the most-refined measuring device in the world, we would still be making an approximate measurement. This is a difficult idea for us to incorporate into our thinking about measurement, because we tend to think of mathematics as an exact science.

Even in the early stages of measuring in non-standard units, young children will encounter this problem and have to find a way of expressing their observations. So they might say 'The book weighs more than 8 marbles but less than 9 marbles', or 'The book weighs a bit more than 8 marbles', or 'The book weighs between 8 and 9 marbles'. These are known technically as *upper and lower bounds* of the measurement.

We have to measure to an appropriate level of *accuracy*. So in measuring age, for example, it is normally appropriate to do this to the year below or the year above. So a child might say 'I'm seven' or 'I'm eight next birthday'. For many purposes we measure time of day to the nearest five minutes, so that we would be amused by someone who said 'I'll meet you at about 4:23 this afternoon', because they appear to be employing an inappropriate level of accuracy. But we would not be amused if a train timetable advertised a departure time of 16:25 and we missed the train because it had left at nearer 16:23.

Consequently, all that we have said earlier about equivalence should be understood in these terms. Phrases such as 'is the same length as' and 'weighs the same as' must be interpreted as implying that the comparison has been made to an appropriate level of accuracy. There is no way in which we can assert that two lines are exactly the same length or that two objects have exactly the same mass.

To sum up, the notions of approximation, upper and lower bounds, and the appropriate level of accuracy are important ideas, fundamental to most aspects of measurement. All these are often underemphasized in work with children.

DIFFERENT TYPES OF MEASURING SCALES

In the final section of this chapter we analyse three different kinds of measuring scales from a mathematical perspective. Length, mass, capacity, time interval, and so on, are examples of what is called a *ratio scale*. Mathematically this is the most sophisticated type of scale. They are called ratio scales because the ratio of two measurements has a real meaning. So, for example, we can compare a length of 90 cm with one of 30 cm either by the difference (60 cm) or by the ratio (3). Hence, using the ratio comparison, we would observe that a length of 90 cm is three times as long as a length of 30 cm, and 90 cm can be made up by combining three lengths of 30 cm.

Similarly, a mass of 100 g is equivalent to ten masses of 10 g, a time interval of 240 minutes can be made up of 6 periods of 40 minutes, and so on. This contrasts with what is called an *interval scale*, such as temperature in degrees celsius (or centigrade), or time of day. To compare a temperature of 30°C with one of 10°C, you can only use the difference (20°C). It makes no sense to talk about one temperature being three times hotter than the other. You cannot make up a temperature of 30°C from three temperatures of 10°C! Similarly, 6 pm is not in any sense three times 2 pm. To compare 6 pm with 2 pm we can only make use of the idea of difference (i.e. it is four hours later), not the idea of ratio.

This contrast between the two types of measuring scale is related to the fact that in a ratio scale the 'zero' is actually 'nothing'. So, a length of 0 cm or a mass of 0 kg is really nothing. But in an interval scale the zero is arbitrary. When the temperature is zero it is not the case that there is no temperature, and time does not disappear when my watch indicates 00:00 at midnight.

Finally, there is what is called an *ordinal scale*. This a measuring scale that makes use of no more than the ordinal aspect of number. We show in Chapter 2 that sometimes numbers are used in just a nominal sense, to label things, and then they are used in an ordinal sense to label things and put them in order. It is in this way that numbers are used in ordinal scales, for example, when measuring how good a hotel is by a system of star ratings, or when measuring performance in an examination by a system of grades, A, B, C, D, E, F. The measurements can be used for no more than comparison by ranking or ordering. We can deduce that a four-star hotel is better than a three-star (and probably more expensive!), and that a grade-B result is better than a grade C, and so on. It certainly makes no sense to use ratios for comparison, as we would with the numbers used for measurements in ratio scales – a four-star hotel is not twice as good as a two-star hotel, whereas a 4-cm rod is twice as long as a 2-cm rod.

And it now makes no sense to talk about the intervals between various measurements, as we would with the numbers used for measurements in interval scales – the difference between an A grade and a B grade is not the same as the difference between a B grade and a C grade, whereas the difference between 1 pm and 2 pm is the same as the difference between 2 pm and 3 pm.

We note, therefore, that we have different types of measuring scales, characterized by different mathematical properties. But what remains throughout, even with ordinal scales, is the ever-present transitive property. We can still conclude that if A is better than B and B is better than C, then A is better than C. For without this property we could not put things in order, and without ordering there would be no measurement.

SUMMARY OF KEY IDEAS IN CHAPTER 5

1. Measurements of length and distance might refer to a wide variety of situations, such as the straight or curved parts of objects, lines drawn on paper, imaginary lines drawn through the air or through objects, straight or curved paths.
2. Volume is the amount of three-dimensional space occupied by an object.
3. Only containers have capacity. The capacity of a container is the volume of liquid it can hold. Capacity and liquid volume are often measured in litres.
4. There are two meanings of time: the time at which an event occurs and the time that something takes to happen.
5. Kilograms and grams are units of mass, not weight. A key phrase for describing the results of weighing is 'weighs the same as' (e.g. the book weighs the same as two hundred grams).
6. Fundamental ideas involved in measurement are comparison and ordering, transitivity, conservation and the idea of a unit.
7. The principle of transitivity is that if A is greater than (less than/equal to) B, and B is greater than (less than/equal to) C, then A must be greater than (less than/equal to) C.
8. Conservation of quantity involves recognizing which transformations (such as pouring a quantity of water into a different-shaped container) preserve which equivalences (e.g. the volume of water stays the same).
9. There are good arguments for introducing children to measuring in units by means of experience, to begin with, of non-standard units.
10. It seems likely that in the UK many Imperial units will survive alongside metric units.
11. The metre, kilogram and second are examples of base units in the SI version of metric units.
12. Prefixes for deriving other units include mega (million), kilo (thousand), hecto (hundred), deci (tenth), centi (hundredth), milli (thousandth) and micro (millionth).
13. Nearly all measurement is approximate.
14. Three different kinds of measuring scales are: ratio scales, such as length and mass, in which measurement can be compared by ratio; interval scales, such as temperature or time of day, in which measurements cannot be compared by ratio, but in which intervals between measurements have meaning; and

ordinal scales, such as exam grades or star ratings, in which measurements can only be compared by ordering.
15. Transitivity applies in all three types of measuring scale.

SOME ACTIVITIES WITH CHILDREN

Activity 5.1: children as non-standard units

Objective To give children experience of measuring lengths and distance using non-standard units, and to explore the effects of using different-sized units.

Materials A class of children; a classroom with walls and tables; sets of any suitable identical objects, such as lolly sticks, bottle tops, rods, cubes, pennies.

Method A group of children stand shoulder to shoulder along one of the classroom walls, from one corner to the other, and another child counts how many children there are. The children are then asked how many would be needed to fill up the opposite wall. A group of children line up shoulder to shoulder to check this. Next they estimate how many children are needed for the length of the other two walls. This is then done and the results recorded.

This is repeated with the children standing with arms outstretched touching finger tips, and again standing in a queue one behind the other as close as they can get. Each time the children are invited beforehand to guess how many will be required.

This experience is extended to estimating distances (from one point to another), as opposed to lengths of actual objects (i.e. the walls). For example, they might estimate the number of children required to stretch diagonally across the room from one corner to the other, again using the three different units (shoulder to shoulder, finger tip to finger tip, and queueing). They might then go into the hall or the playground and try this with the distances between two chairs placed in various positions.

All this should be followed by discussion about what is discovered. The children could next undertake a similar exploration on their table tops (width, length, diagonal distance) using a variety of non-standard units, such as lolly sticks, bottle tops, and so on.

Activity 5.2: estimation challenge

Objective To familiarize children with the sizes of some standard units of measurement.

Materials 30-cm ruler; scrap paper; something to act as a small screen (e.g. a large book); plastic pennies as prizes.

Method This is a simple but effective game for a small group of children. Players take turns to draw on a piece of scrap paper a line of any number of centimetres length they wish, using the ruler. They do this behind the screen, so that the others cannot see them doing it. The line is then shown and each of the other players estimates how long it is. One player should write down their estimates. They then check the length of the line with the ruler, and the player (or players) getting nearest wins a penny. You win a bonus penny if you get the length spot on.

Variations of this game suggest themselves: for example, children could use a balance to weigh out quantities of sand into a yoghurt pot (using 10-g masses only) again behind a screen. Others have to estimate the mass.

Activity 5.3: short straws

Objective To give children experience related to the concept of conservation of length.

Materials A supply of cheap straws, or strips of thin card; scissors; a screen, as in Activity 5.2.

Method This is a simple game for four players. In turn each player takes a set of three straws all the same length and then, using the scissors, shortens one slightly. The three straws are presented to the others in a fist in the traditional fashion, trying to disguise which one is shorter than the others. Each chooses one straw. The loser keeps the short straw, which counts as a point against. At the end of the game the player with the least number of short straws is the winner.

The intention is that young children will, through this game, experience the idea that the length of an object is not changed by its being displaced.

Activity 5.4: conservation game (volume and mass)

Objective To give children experience related to the concept of conservation of mass and volume.

Materials A number of different-shaped, clear, plastic or glass containers and measuring jars, and a small cup; a supply of water; three identical non-transparent containers with lids (e.g. yoghurt pots); a supply of sand; a balance; a ball-bearing.

Method This is another game for four players, in two teams of two. Team A measures out the same quantity of water into three clear containers, and then adds one extra cupful of water to one of them. While they are doing this, team B measures out the same mass of sand into the three pots, buries the ball-bearing in one of them and replaces the lids.

They challenge each other to identify the odd one out. Team B is allowed only to look at the containers of water. Team A is allowed to pick up, but not to rattle vigorously the pots of sand. After they have made their judgements each team can check to see if they are right, by pouring water or by balancing pots. They then swap over and repeat the experiment with team A doing mass and team B doing volume.

Activity 5.5: investigating ordering

Objective To give children experience of transitivity and ordering.
Materials

1. A set of cards with events of the day written or depicted on them – alarm goes off, get up, have breakfast, etc.
2. A collection of bottles and jars.
3. A balance and a set of identical-looking sealed containers or parcels, filled with a variety of materials, such as sand, sawdust, ball-bearings.
4. A list of tasks taking various amounts of time (count to a hundred, tie up your shoe laces, do ten press-ups, etc.).

Method The children are to find a strategy for ordering three or more items. In each case they should start with three and order these. Then extend to four, five, six, etc.

1. The children have to put the events of the day in order from earliest to latest. To start with any three cards can be used. A nice touch is to have letters written on the backs of the cards, so that when the whole set is finally ordered they can be turned over to reveal a message such as '*well done*'.
2. Using the balance the children order three containers by mass. Gradually extend this by adding a fourth container, a fifth, and so on.
3. By pouring water from one bottle to another, children explore the same problem with capacity.
4. Two children perform two of the tasks starting at the same time, and discover which takes the longer and which takes the shorter time. Eventually they must order the whole list from the one taking the least amount of time to the one taking the greatest.

Activity 5.6: snail race

Objective To give children some concept of a time interval of one minute.
Materials A stop clock.
Method This is a bit of fun for a class of children learning about time. The class is taken into the hall or on to the playground, where starting and finishing lines

are marked out. All watches must be removed beforehand. The children line up at the start and 'race' to the finish. The winner is the child who crosses the line nearest to exactly one minute after the start! The teacher stands on the finishing line and makes a mental note of the child crossing the line at the appropriate moment, but lets the rest finish. All competitors must keep moving. Have several heats and then a final. Discuss after each heat whether most people were too slow or too fast.

Activity 5.7: ordering packets

Objective More experience of ordering, and to heighten children's awareness of measurement in the world outside school.

Materials Children to collect as many different empty packets where the contents are marked in grams or kilograms.

Method Along the whole length of a wall, make a number-line frieze, marked from 0 to 2,000 g. As packets are collected, children display them on the appropriate part of the number line. Write the number of grams in large numerals underneath. The children should be challenged to find packets with different numbers of grams from those already displayed.

Activity 5.8: metric or Imperial?

Objective To make explicit to children the mixture of units in use in everyday life.

Materials Whatever can be collected in the way of packets, notices, advertisements, newspaper cuttings, in which measurements of various sorts appear.

Method The children to make a display of the materials collected. Arrange these in a set diagram, as shown in Figure 5.6, to show which ones use just metric units, which use just Imperial units, and which use both.

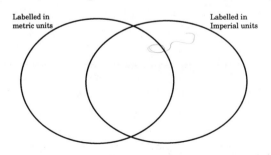

Figure 5.6 Set diagram for Activity 5.8

SUGGESTIONS FOR FURTHER READING

Glenn, J.A. (ed.) 1980 *Children Learning to Measure: A Handbook for Teachers*, Harper & Row, London. (This book offers imaginative, step-by-step suggestions for developing the necessary skills and concepts relating to measurement.)

Jarvis, T. (1988) 'Weight and see', *Junior Education*, August, pp. 30–1. (Jarvis provides many practical examples – including children making their own balances – that helped promote her pupils understanding of the concept of weight.)

Johnson, G.L. (1987) 'Using a metric unit to help preservice teachers appreciate the value of manipulative materials', *Arithmetic Teacher*, Vol. 35, no. 2, pp. 14–20. (An article that provides useful strategies for developing a practical appreciation of the metric units used to measure length, area, volume, capacity and weight.)

Kerslake, D. (1975) 'Taking time out', *Mathematics Teaching*, Vol. 73, pp. 8–10. (In this short paper, Kerslake discusses the complexities involved in understanding the concept of time.)

Kerslake, D. (1976) 'Volume and capacity', *Mathematics Teaching*, Vol. 77, pp. 14–15. (Kerslake offers suggestions for a scheme of work concerning volume and capacity that she considers suitable for the 5–11-year-old age-range.)

6
SHAPE AND SPACE

It is at first sight a little surprising that two activities as apparently different as arithmetic and geometry should form the two prongs of a single subject called mathematics. Although both number work and shape and spatial work may appear in the mathematics scheme or syllabus, teachers of young children would often regard them as very different kinds of activity. The proposals for the mathematics national curriculum for England and Wales underline this view, with knowledge, skills and understanding of number, algebra and measures forming one profile component, and knowlege, skills and understanding of shape and space appearing in another. This is a recognition that performances in these two areas are likely to be very different for individual children. This is hardly surprising from a psychological point of view, since the manipulation of number is essentially an activity that involves the left hemisphere of the brain, whereas spatial thinking functions through the right hemisphere. So why do we regard them as components of one discipline?

- I never think of them as being the same subject. Number work and shape are quite distinct as far as I'm concerned.
- When you're doing something like measuring area the two things come together. That's shape and number work.
- It's something to do with pattern, isn't it? You get patterns in number and patterns in shape.

A simple game, called 'Guess my rule', which can be played with either numbers or shapes, demonstrates some underlying ideas shared by these two aspects of mathematics.

In this game one person challenges the other players to guess the rule they have in their mind. In the number version, the players suggest various numbers to

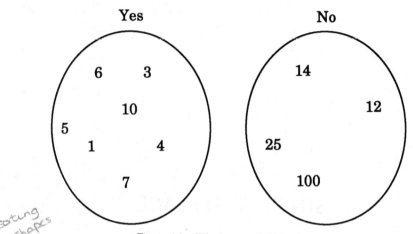

Figure 6.1   What's my rule? Numbers

which the challenger responds 'yes' or 'no', depending on whether or not the rule is satisfied. As they are called out the numbers are written in either the 'yes' set or the 'no' set. For example, after several suggestions something like Figure 6.1 might have been written on the board. By this stage someone may be able to articulate the rule being used, namely 'less than eleven'.

The situation we have here can be analysed using the notions of equivalence and transformation that have appeared throughout this book. The numbers in the 'yes' set in Figure 6.1 are different, but there is something that is the same about them, something that for the purpose of this game makes them equivalent. They are all less than eleven. You could focus on various attributes of the numbers in this set, such as noticing that six is bigger than five, or that six is twice three, and so on. But you have to ignore all such observations of how the numbers are different from each other in favour of the one thing that they have in common.

A similar game can be played with a set of shapes, either three-dimensional solid shapes or two-dimensional plane shapes. The set of shapes is set out on a table and once again the challenger uses a rule to sort them into a 'yes' set and a 'no' set. After a while, in a game using a set of cut-out card shapes, the situation shown in Figure 6.2 might have arisen. In identifying the rule as 'four-sided', the same sort of thinking is involved here as with the number game. The shapes in the 'yes' set are all different from one another, but we are recognizing them as being in some sense the same. As our eye sweeps from one shape to the other, we ignore all the transformations taking place and concentrate on the equivalence.

It is our contention that the mathematical notions of transformation and equivalence are fundamental to both number and shape activities, and it is this

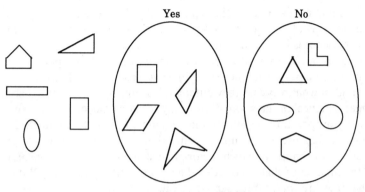

Figure 6.2   What's my rule? Shapes

that makes these two areas into a unified subject. We have seen right from our earliest discussions in this book that these ideas are at the heart of mathematical thinking. In chapter 1 we show that a statement such as '3 + 5 = 8' could be viewed both as a statement about a transformation being applied to the 3 and the 5, and to an equivalence that emerges. In Chapter 2 we show that the concept of a cardinal number could be analysed in terms of recognizing what is the same about a number of sets of different objects; in other words, recognizing an equivalence. In Chapter 5, we show that these ideas of transformation and equivalence are the basis of the notion of conservation in measurement. In this final chapter we use these two concepts to analyse geometrical experiences, concentrating particularly on two-dimensional shapes. Many of the ideas discussed can be applied equally well to three-dimensional shapes, but the analysis becomes more complex.

- But a lot of the schemes seem to start with three-dimensional shapes, cubes and cuboids and things like that.
- I find that the children come to school already knowing a lot of the words for flat shapes, like square and circle.
- What's the argument for starting with three-dimensional? Wouldn't it be simpler to start with two-dimensional and build up?
- But they live in a three-dimensional world and are used to handling three-dimensional objects, like boxes and tins and toys. You should start with three-dimensional things you can pick up and handle, and move down to the two-dimensional shapes.
- A lot of my children call a cuboid an oblong anyway.

It seems clear to us that two-dimensional and three-dimensional experiences – flat shapes and solid shapes – need to go hand in hand. Of course, children do live in a three-dimensional world of solid shapes, but in order to describe, identify and classify these shapes, we have to focus on the shapes of their surfaces. Hence the confusion between a cuboid and an oblong. And we should bear in mind that, even before they come to school, children will have spent a lot of time looking at pictures in books and at television screens, so that much of their experience is in fact two-dimensional.

Hence, in our analysis of geometric thinking we shall compare sets of two-dimensional shapes, each time asking in what sense are the shapes in the set the same, and in what ways are they different. The analysis is structured according to a mathematical progression, using a way of classifying geometric experiences originally proposed by a German mathematician, Felix Klein, in 1872. In our analysis we shall use one geometric shape, that shown in Figure 6.3, to generate further sets of shapes, in which the original shape is distorted more and more, until the final set of shapes considered have very little in common. But we shall see that they are still in some sense equivalent.

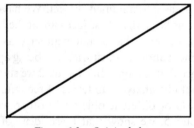

Figure 6.3   Original shape

This analysis helps us to see that sometimes we, as teachers, expect children to focus on the ways in which things are different, and at other times to focus on the ways in which they are the same. It seems as though learning geometry is a matter of picking up clues as to what you are expected to ignore and what you are expected to take into account on any particular occasion!

In the course of our analysis of geometry we shall identify some of the mathematical concepts needed to discuss the samenesses and differences involved. In this way we hope teachers will see (1) how the fundamental ideas of transformation and equivalence underpin almost all geometric experiences, and (2) how the various concepts children encounter in shape and spatial activities fit into a coherent mathematical system. Thus, by making such connections as these we hope that teachers will feel that their own understanding of the geometric experiences they present to young children has been enhanced.

TRANSLATION

Consider the set of shapes shown in Figure 6.4. Are they the same shape?

• They look identical to me.

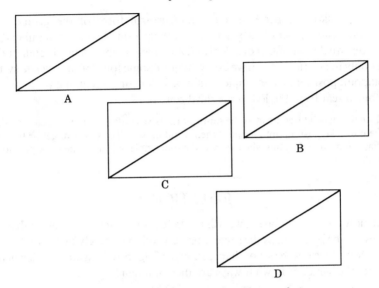

Figure 6.4   A set of shapes produced by translations

- But they're not exactly the same, are they? They're like identical twins. They look alike in every respect but they are different people.
- They've got different names as well. This one's called A and that one's called B.
- They're drawn in different places on the page.

We had better start by noting that when we draw, for example, a 'rectangle' on a piece of paper, or on a page of a book, then we are only drawing an approximate representation of an abstract mathematical idea. This abstract idea is a four-sided figure, consisting of lines of no thickness, meeting at right angles at points of no area. So in our discussion about sameness and difference we are not concerned with the actual molecules of ink constituting the drawing on the paper, but with the abstraction this represents. We will disregard questions such as whether the thickness of the lines in the various shapes are exactly the same, and questions relating to the approximate nature of all measurement. With these provisos we could then conclude that the shapes in this set are the same in every respect except one. They are all rectangles with a diagonal drawn from the bottom left- to top right-hand corner, they are the same dimensions, the angles are the same, corresponding sides point in the same direction, and so on. But they differ in that each one is drawn in a different *position*.

The transformation that changes one of these shapes into any other one in the set is called a *translation*. This is a sliding, without turning, from one position to another. To describe such translations we need concepts of *direction*, such as *up*, *down*, *left*, and *right*.

Young children experience a one-dimensional form of the geometry of translations and position when they move up and down the number line. However, we do not often consider solid and plane shapes to be different if they differ only in position. When we do, we require some form of *co-ordinate* system to pinpoint position. An example would be in locating a seat in a room as, say, the fourth seat from the left in the third row.

> If we tell the children to sit at the same tables as yesterday, then we would be asking them to take position into account then, wouldn't we? The tables might be the same shape and same size, but when we say 'the same table' we mean the same position as well.

ROTATION

From now on in our anlaysis, we will not take position into account, so that two shapes will be regarded as the same if one is produced merely by translating the other. Now consider the set of shapes shown in Figure 6.5. Again we ask whether they are the same, or in what ways are they different?

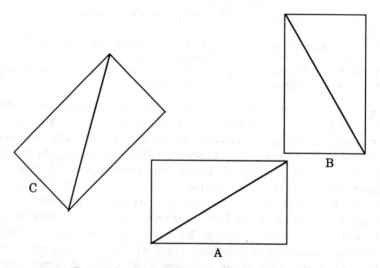

Figure 6.5   A set of shapes produced by rotations

- They are the same shape, but they have been turned through various angles.
- We have examples like this in our maths scheme where the children have to colour in shapes that are the same.
- Some children find it very hard to realize that a cuboid is the same if it's standing up or on its side.

Again we see that in many contexts we would regard the shapes in Figure 6.5 as being the same shape. The difference now is that they are oriented in space differently – corresponding lines in the shapes point in different directions. To move from one shape to another the transformation applied is called a *rotation*.

In order to take into account this particular transformation, the geometric concept required is that of *angle*. There are basically two ways of thinking about the concept of angle, one dynamic and the other static. Here we are using the *dynamic* aspect: an angle as a measure of the amount of turn or rotation that has occurred. For example, the transformation from A to B in Figure 6.5 is a rotation through a quarter-turn.

To be more precise about a rotation, we might also need to specify whether it is *clockwise* or *anticlockwise*. The rotation from A to B in Figure 6.5 could be a quarter-turn anticlockwise. A quarter-turn is also called a *right angle*. This is shorthand for upright angle. This is the angle that a stick turns through when you move it from flat on the ground to an upright position.

Sometimes a shape does not change when it is rotated through certain angles. For example, the diagram in Figure 6.6 can be rotated through a half-turn (two

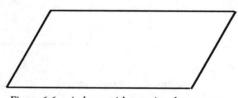

Figure 6.6   A shape with rotational symmetry

right angles) and it would look the same. To convince yourself of this just turn the book upside down. While you've got the book upside down you might decide whether some letters of the alphabet, such as S, A, C or N, have this same geometric property.

This property is called *rotational symmetry*. In their practical explorations with two-dimensional shapes, young children can experience this property by drawing a box round a shape and then seeing how many different ways the shape will fit into its box, without picking it up and turning it over. They experience the same idea when posting shapes through holes in the post-box toy. Some shapes can be rotated into a number of different positions in which they fit into their holes. A shape without rotational symmetry is the hardest to do, because it will fit through its hole in only one way. We should make clear that we are not suggesting that young children should necessarily be taught to analyse shapes in terms of this concept of rotational symmetry. But we hope that their teachers' awareness of this concept might help them to identify the relevance of some of the informal practical explorations in which young children might engage –

moving shapes around, drawing round them, fitting them into boxes, and so on – as the basis for geometric analysis at a later stage.

REFLECTION

From now on in our analysis, we do not take into account changes in position or orientation. The result of translating or rotating a shape will be regarded as the same shape. We now turn our attention to the two shapes shown in Figure 6.7, and again ask in what sense are they the same shape, and in what ways are they different.

- They're different because they're mirror images of each other.
- It's like a pair of shoes. They're the same in one sense, but they're different because one's for the left foot and the other for the right foot.

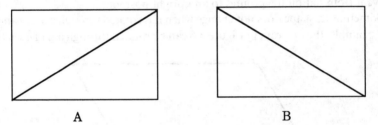

A   B

Figure 6.7   Mirror images

Again we have a situation where for many purposes we would regard shapes as being the same, yet on other occasions we would focus on the differences. When you look in a mirror and comb your hair you are making use of the equivalence between yourself and your mirror image. When you choose a pair of shoes from the heap in the bottom of your wardrobe you look for two that are the same as each other, but then when you have to decide which shoe goes on which foot you focus on the difference between them.

The transformation that would change one of the shapes in Figure 6.7 into the other is called a *reflection*. Associated with each reflection is a *mirror line*. The reader can no doubt imagine where a mirror could be placed in Figure 6.7, in order that one of the shapes becomes the mirror image of the other.

To take into account the changes produced by reflections, the concepts of *left* and *right* are particularly important. Thus when you look into the mirror and raise your right arm, the person in the mirror raises their left arm. It is important to note that 'left and right' are different kinds of ideas from 'up and down'. Up is the same direction for all of us, all the time. But left for me might be right for you, and what is on my left now might be on my right when I move to a new position.

- It's as though you have to learn the conventions. Sometimes in maths lessons we ask children to pick out the same shape, and expect them to regard mirror images as the same, but then we correct them when they don't distinguish between the letter d and the letter b!

Sometimes a shape does not change when it is reflected. For example, the mirror image of the diagram in Figure 6.8 would look the same. To convince yourself of this, look at the diagram in a mirror, or hold the book up to the light

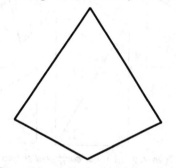

Figure 6.8   A shape with line symmetry

and look through the other side of the page. Remember that we are disregarding changes produced by translating or rotating the book. While you're doing one of these you might investigate whether any of the letters of the alphabet, such as S, A, C or N, have this geometric property.

This property is called *line symmetry*. In their practical explorations with two-dimensional shapes, young children can experience this property in a number of different ways. They can draw a box round a shape and then investigate whether the shape will fit into its box when it is picked up and turned over. Or they can cut out a shape and discover whether it can be folded along a line so that one half matches the other half. Such a fold line is called a *line of symmetry*. The two halves are mirror images of each other, with the line of symmetry as a mirror line. They can experiment with looking at shapes in mirrors, and seeing what happens when a mirror is placed along a line of symmetry. Another useful experience is to copy shapes on to tracing-paper and then to compare the original with the shape that appears on the reverse side of the paper.

SIMILARITY

If we now decide to disregard translations, rotations and reflections, when comparing shapes, then we would consider all the shapes in Figure 6.9 to be the same. Mathematicians would say that these shapes are *congruent*.

Figure 6.10 introduces a further way in which shapes may change, while still

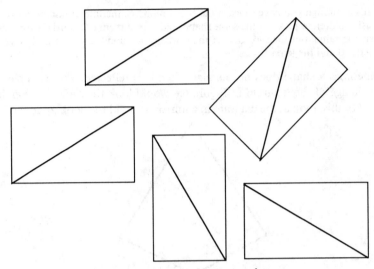

Figure 6.9　A set of congruent shapes

in some senses staying the same. Now the sizes of the shapes are different, but we would still in many contexts regard them as the same shape.

- It's like when the children are working with Logiblocs. They sometimes put the large triangles and small triangles into the same set, and sometimes into different sets.

The transformation being applied now is technically called a *similarity* and the shapes are said to be *similar*. This is, of course, using the word 'similar' in a precise technical sense, not in the colloquial sense where you might say that your brother or sister and yourself have similar looks. We can think of a similarity as being either a *scaling up* or a *scaling down*. We're talking about what happens, for example, when we use a photocopier to enlarge or reduce something. The key concept required to specify a scaling is that of *scale factor*. In Figure 6.10, for example, B is the result of scaling A by a scale factor of 2. The effect of this is to multiply the lengths of all the sides by 2, using the scale-factor model of multiplication discussed in Chapter 4. Since all the lengths are scaled by the same factor, the ratio of any two lengths in the shape remains the same. Compare the example of a percentage pay rise, given in Chapter 4, where all salaries are scaled by the same factor, in order to preserve the ratios between salaries.

Children experience scaling in model cars, dolls and dolls' houses, play houses, maps and plans, scale drawings, photographs, and so on.

- One of my boys measured the playground to make a plan, then said he couldn't do it. He said the paper wasn't big enough, because it was only about one metre long, but the playground was thirty metres!

- I get my class to make a larger version of a small picture, by drawing a grid over it and copying it onto a larger grid.
- We were reading a book about a monster and there was this picture of a huge foot next to a small man. None of my children got it. They didn't seem to appreciate the significance of scale at all.

Once again we note that there are times when we focus on the transformation, and expect children to take differences in size into account, and times when we focus on the equivalence, disregarding the difference in scale.

I was doing some work on halves and put a big drawing of a square on the board. I asked the children to copy it onto their paper. Afterwards it struck me as interesting that they all quite happily chose to ignore the size of the square. And that's what I meant them to do as well, since I hadn't given them a piece of paper big enough to copy my square anyway!

Under a scaling, the angles in a shape remain unchanged. We are using the word *angle* here in its *static* sense. This is a measure of the difference in direction

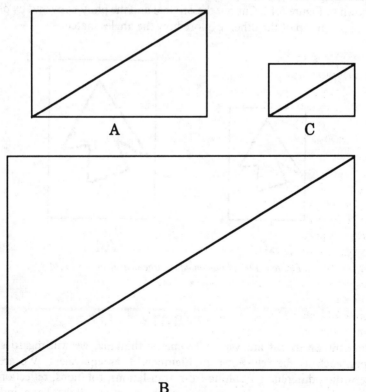

Figure 6.10   A set of shapes produced by scaling

between two lines. So the angle X in Figure 6.11 is smaller than the angle Y, because the difference in the direction of the two lines meeting at X is smaller than that of the two lines meeting at Y.

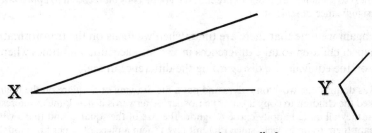

Figure 6.11   Which angle is smaller?

One way to become explicitly aware of what remains the same under a scaling is to make a photocopy enlargement of a drawing, say, from A5 size paper to A4, as shown in Figure 6.12. Cut out the original and the photocopy and by placing one shape on top of the other, explore how the angles match.

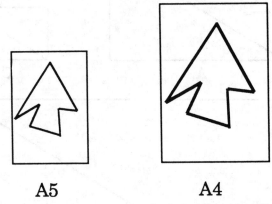

A5   A4

Figure 6.12   Photocopied enlargement from A5 to A4

AFFINITY

From now on in our analysis of geometric thinking, we will regard similar shapes, such as the set shown in Figure 6.13, as equivalent. We are now disregarding differences resulting from translations, rotations, reflections and scalings. As far as we are concerned, from this point on, all the shapes in Figure 6.13 are the same shape.

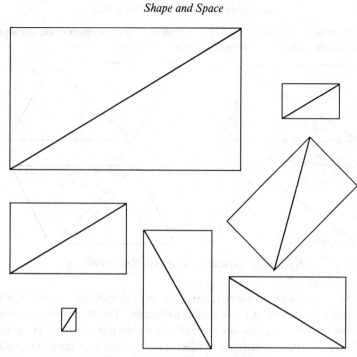

Figure 6.13　A set of similar shapes

Now consider the set of shapes shown in Figure 6.14. Although our original shape has changed quite considerably, we might still recognize that there is something the same about all the shapes in Figure 6.14. Even though the shapes are not geometrically similar, there is still a *family likeness*, some shared properties that lead us on some occasions to ignore the differences between the members of the family. We might select them from a collection of shapes, recognizing an equivalence, and distinguishing them from other shapes that do not share the family likeness.

- My children were doing an exercise in the maths scheme where they had to colour

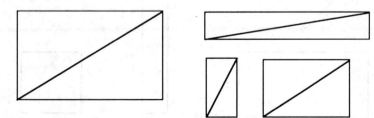

Figure 6.14　A set of shapes with a family likeness

in the cuboids on a shelf. One of them coloured in the shelf, because she said that was a cuboid as well! I thought that was very clever.

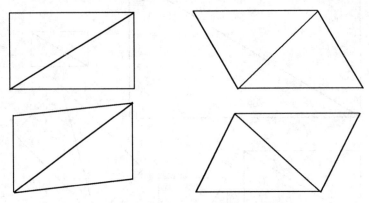

Figure 6.15   Another example of a family likeness

Figure 6.15 provides another example of a set of shapes, including our original shape, which share one of these family likenesses. The technical word for the transformation that changes our original shape into one of the others in the set is an *affinity*. The precise analysis of these transformations is fairly involved and not particularly helpful for a teacher of young children. But we may notice that the shapes in Figures 6.14 and 6.15 have been produced by stretching or shearing the original. In order to recognize equivalences of this sort, we need particularly the concept of *parallel*. Two lines are parallel if they are pointing in the same direction. One condition of an affinity is that parallel lines must stay parallel.

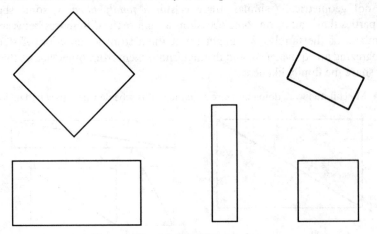

Figure 6.16   A family of rectangles

Within the set of *polygons* (two-dimensional shapes with straight edges), we can identify sets of shapes such as triangles (three sided), quadrilaterals (four sided), pentagons (five sided), hexagons (six sided), and so on. The set of quadrilaterals contains some particularly interesting examples of affinities. For example, there is the family known as *rectangles*, shown in Figure 6.16, which share the property that all four angles are right angles.

- Aren't some of those squares, not rectangles?
- Why has the word oblong gone out of fashion?

There is a small confusion here that often arises. A square is a member of the set of rectangles, since it shares the family likeness, having all four angles as right angles. It is, in fact, a special sort of rectangle, since all the sides are equal. If we want to distinguish between squares and other rectangles then we can refer to *square rectangles* and *oblong rectangles*. This confusion is reinforced if we refer to the pieces in the Logiblocks set as squares and rectangles.

A second important family of quadrilaterals is the set of *parallelograms*, some examples of which are shown in Figure 6.17. These share the property that two pairs of opposite sides are parallel.

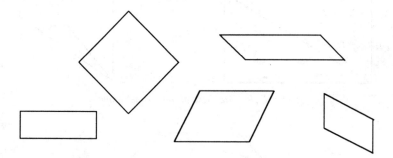

Figure 6.17   A family of parallelograms

- So a rectangle is a parallelogram.
- And since a square is a special sort of rectangle, it must be a special sort of parallelogram as well.
- What's a rhombus?

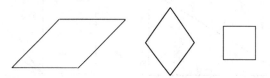

Figure 6.18   A family of rhombuses

This leads to one last example of an affinity. The set of *rhombuses*, some examples of which are shown in Figure 6.18, are parallelograms with all four sides equal in length. We can imagine the affinity involved here as taking a square of any size, hinged at the corners, and then transforming it by tilting it to one side or the other.

PERSPECTIVITY

In the previous section we identify some examples of families of shapes, such as rectangles, parallelograms and rhombuses, which can be considered as equivalent because they share some particular property. But would we ever recognize the shapes shown in Figure 6.19 as being the same? In fact, we

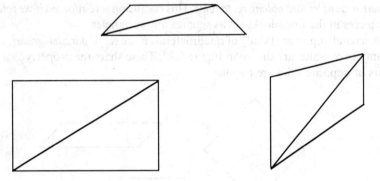

Figure 6.19   Are these all the 'same' shape?

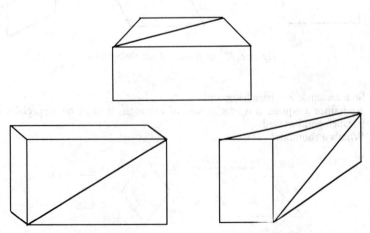

Figure 6.20   Perspective drawings of the same shape

apparently recognize these shapes as being the same all the time as we move around our three-dimensional world, since these are merely *perspective* drawings of the same shape. If we imagine our original shape drawn on the side of a box, then the other shapes in Figure 6.19 are simply representations of how the shape might appear to us as we turn the box round and view it from different angles, as illustrated in Figure 6.20.

The analysis of perspectivity is a particularly difficult piece of mathematics, which should not detain us now. But it is interesting for us to observe that when

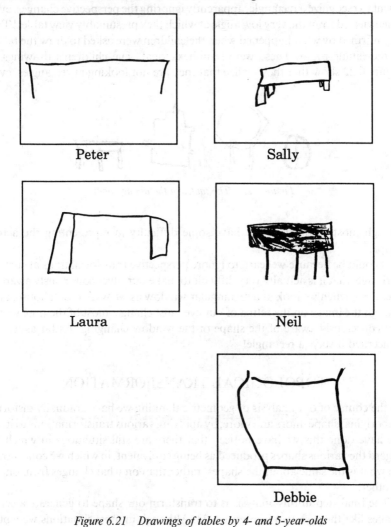

Figure 6.21 Drawings of tables by 4- and 5-year-olds

we learn to recognize shapes viewed from different perspectives in our three-dimensional world, then we are learning to ignore the changes in the shape associated with the perspective transformation.

One teacher asked her 4- and 5-year-olds to draw a table. Figure 6.21 provides some typical examples of their drawings. About half of the children drew a side view of the table, like those of Peter and Laura. But the other half drew what was basically a rectangle, with some legs attached somewhere, like those of Sally, Neil and Debbie. It is fascinating to note that even such young children have already learnt to recognize a rectangle, apparently ignoring the perspective changes, even when viewed from the very low angle at which they presumably view tables! This is confirmed by what happened when the children were asked to draw the tables in the dining-room. These were semi-hexagonal. The children's drawings in Figure 6.22 show that they realize that they are not looking at rectangles, even

Figure 6.22   The tables in the dining-room

though most of them clearly have some difficulty in representing the actual shape.

It could be because we learn to ignore perspective transformations at such an early age, that it is actually very difficult to make ourselves consciously aware of them. So, when we look at a rectangular window as we walk past a house, even though the image on the retina of our eye must change, most of the time we are not consciously aware of the shape of the window changing. As far as we are concerned it stays a rectangle!

TOPOLOGICAL TRANSFORMATION

In the course of our analysis of geometric thinking we have gradually distorted our original shape, more and more, by applying various transformations to it. As we have done this we have noticed that there are still situations in which we regard the various shapes produced as being equivalent, in which we concentrate on what is the same about the shapes, rather than on what changes from one to another.

The final step in this analysis is to transform our shape to generate a set of shapes like those shown in Figure 6.23. Although in most situations we would

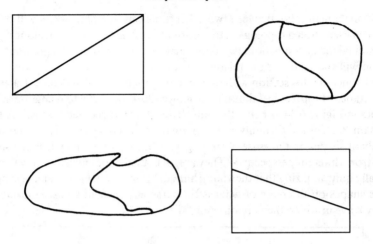

Figure 6.23   Are these in any sense the 'same' shape?

regard these as being different shapes, we may still recognize something about them that makes them equivalent. In fact, if these diagrams were representing pieces of wire constituting electrical circuits then clearly they would all be the same circuit.

To generate each of the shapes in Figure 6.23 we have applied a *topological transformation* to the original shape. In a transformation of this sort, the shape can be pulled, stretched or distorted in any way you like, provided that no lines are broken or joined in the process. Clearly none of our usual geometric properties – such as length, angle, parallelism, ratio of lengths, the number of sides, or even the straightness of sides – is preserved under such transformations. But if we think of a two-dimensional shape as a network of *paths*, enclosing *regions*, meeting at *junctions*, then we can see that all the shapes in Figure 6.23 are the same. Each is a network of three paths from one junction to another, enclosing two regions.

This indicates that it is often essentially topological thinking that is involved in giving directions for a route. 'Go out of the drive, turn left, then the second on the right, just past the post box, carry on until you come to a roundabout, take the second exit, ...'. A route can be described like this, without any reference to distance, scale or direction, but simply referring to a network of paths and junctions, to what is passed on a particular path and whether you turn left or right at any particular junction. A useful topological exercise for children is to articulate their route from home to school.

Some of the most fundamental geometric ideas are those preserved under a topological transformation: ideas such as *between, next, meet, inside* and *outside*.

So, if one junction lies between two other junctions in a network, it will still lie between them after a topological transformation. The next junction along a path will still be the next junction; two paths that meet will still meet; a point inside a region will still be inside the region, and so on.

We conclude this section with one final observation, which demonstrates the importance of topological thinking. Young children are able to recognize all the shapes in Figure 6.24 as being the same letter. In what geometric sense are they the same? They are certainly not congruent, or even similar. They are not a family of shapes, in the sense of sharing an affinity, nor are they just one shape seen from different perspectives. They are, of course, topologically equivalent. It is really quite amazing that the young human brain is capable of categorizing all these shapes on the basis of what is the same about them whilst ignoring the many ways in which they are different.

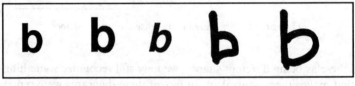

Figure 6.24   A set of topologically-equivalent shapes

The children's drawings of semi-hexagonal tables in Figure 6.22, like their drawings of people's faces, are also essentially topological representations of the shapes they observe. They are certainly not congruent, similar or drawn in perspective. Only in a topological sense are the drawings equivalent to the objects they represent. This suggests that this is in fact the most basic concept of sameness that forms a starting-point for geometric thinking. From this basis we have to provide a range of practical experiences of shapes – picking them up and looking at them from different angles, drawing round them, cutting them out, moving them round, fitting them in boxes, matching them, comparing them, contrasting them, scaling them, looking at them in mirrors, turning them over, folding them, rotating them, fitting them together, sorting them into families, and so on and so on – in order to equip the children with the language, skills and concepts needed to recognize the full range of equivalences outlined in this chapter. For it is this recognition of what stays the same when things change that is the basis of understanding of shape and space.

SUMMARY OF KEY IDEAS IN CHAPTER 6

1. Geometrical thinking involves recognizing both transformations and equi-valences: ways in which shapes differ and ways in which they can be regarded as being the same.

2. Transformations that might be applied, in order of increasing distortion of the original shape, are translation, rotation, reflection, similarity, affinity, perspectivity and topological transformation.

3. Geometric concepts needed to identify and discuss transformations and equivalences in shape and space include position, direction, up, down, left, right, co-ordinates, clockwise, anticlockwise, angle (dynamic and static), right angle, rotational symmetry, mirror line, line symmetry, congruent, similar, scale factor, scaling up, scaling down, family likeness, parallel, polygon, side, triangle, quadrilateral, pentagon, hexagon, etc., square rectangles and oblong rectangles, parallelogram, rhombus, perspective drawing, path, region, junction, between, next, meet, inside, outside.

SOME ACTIVITIES WITH CHILDREN

The main text of this chapter contains a number of suggestions of the sorts of practical activities in which children might engage in order to experience some of the fundamental geometric ideas discussed. The shape-sorting game, 'what's my rule?', is a good starting-point for any series of lessons on shape. Teachers might also, for example, wish to get children to explore rotational and line symmetry by cutting out shapes, drawing round them, looking at them in mirrors, and so on. Or they might experiment with making photocopy enlargements and reductions of children's drawings and getting the children to cut them out and investigate the relationships. Teachers of young children will find it instructive to analyse their drawings of three-dimensional objects such as in the table-drawing example discussed in this chapter.

We conclude with a few further suggestions for practical activities.

Activity 6.1: what are my rules?

Objective To give children further experience of sorting shapes according to their properties.

Materials A set of two- or three-dimensional shapes; and a network diagram as illustrated in Figure 6.25.

Method This is played like 'what's my rule?', but this time the challenger has two rules. The shapes are taken along the network and sorted into four sets, according to two rules, turning left at a junction if the shape satisfies the rule, and right if it does not. Once some shapes have been sorted the other children have to predict which way a given shape will go at each junction. Eventually the rules must be articulated and checked.

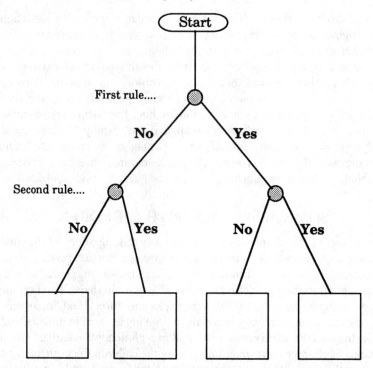

Figure 6.25   Network diagram for 'what are my rules?' (Activity 6.1)

Activity 6.2: shapes in the environment

Objective To heighten children's awareness of shapes used in the world around them.

Materials A street for each child with drawings of shapes, as shown in Figure 6.26.

Method The children explore an area outside looking for examples of the shapes illustrated. When they find them they tick them off (or if they have watches they could write down the time at which they found the shape). The sheet illustrated in Figure 6.26 has been used by hundreds of children on a mathematics trail around the University of East Anglia.

Activity 6.3: dismantling boxes

Objective To help children to identify the plane shapes forming the constituent parts of solid shapes.

Materials Collect two each of any interesting-shaped boxes from your shopping – pyramids, cylinders, tetrahedra, cubes, cuboids, prisms are all quite common. Children can bring in examples.

Method The children should go round the edges of one of the boxes in each pair with a thick, black, marker-pen. Then they dismantle this box, and cut out and identify the shapes that have been marked out, discarding the flaps. The other box in the pair and the cut-out shapes are mounted in a display, to highlight the various flat surfaces used to make the solid shape, as illustrated in Figure 6.27.

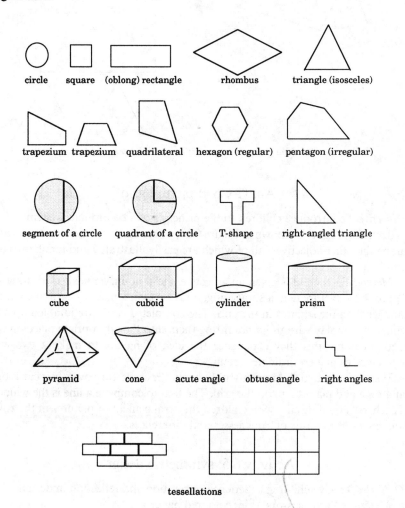

Figure 6.26 Shapes in the environment (Activity 6.2)

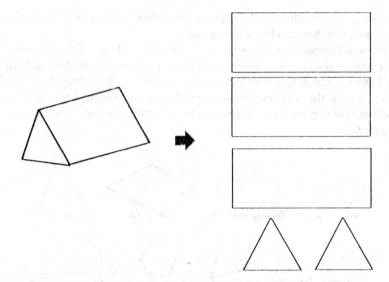

Figure 6.27   Identifying the flat surfaces in solid shapes (Activity 6.3)

Activity 6.4: picture grid

Objective To introduce children to the principle of a co-ordinate system.

Materials A grid, as shown in Figure 6.28, where along one axis are nouns and along the other adjectives, all of which are easily illustrated and familiar to the children.

Method Each child is given an adjective and a noun, and asked to draw an appropriate picture (e.g. a spotty dog, a fat car), on a piece of card just a little smaller than the squares in the grid. The completed cards are jumbled up and children can play various games fitting them into the appropriate place on the grid. In doing this they experience the idea of having to make a two-way reference, as in a co-ordinate system.

For example, two children might share out the cards, turn over their cards one at a time and place them on the grid. The first to complete a line is the winner. Teachers should discuss with children the arrangement of pictures in the rows and columns in terms of samenesses and differences.

Activity 6.5: symmetric designs

Objective To give children experience of rotation and reflection in design.

Materials Card; scissors; thin, coloured paper.

Method Each child draws a shape of their own choosing on card. This is then

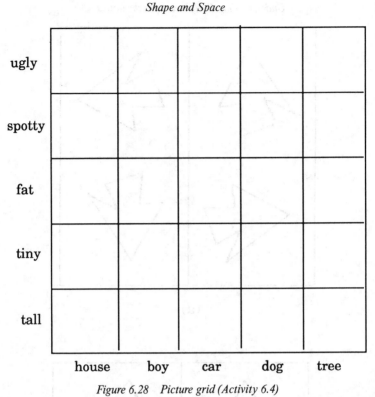

Figure 6.28 Picture grid (Activity 6.4)

cut out and used as a template to reproduce eight copies of the shape in coloured paper. These copies are used to make two attractive designs, as illustrated in Figure 6.29 (a) and (b). The original shape is put in the top-left corner. Then in (a) the shape is rotated each time into a new position, and in (b) it is reflected each time. Children should talk with their teachers about the relationships displayed in their designs, using the language of same and different.

Activity 6.6: odd one out

Objective To provide experience of transformation and equivalence in shape and space.

Materials The teacher prepares several examples of strips of sets of shapes, as shown in Figure 6.30; blank strips for children to use.

Method The strips are shown to the children, who have to identify the odd one out, and explain why. For example, in (b) the second drawing is the odd one out because it is a mirror image. The children can then make up their own set of

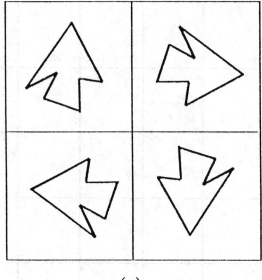

(a)

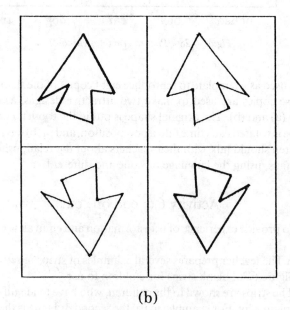

(b)

Figure 6.29   Symmetric designs produced (a) By rotation, (b) By reflection (Activity 6.5)

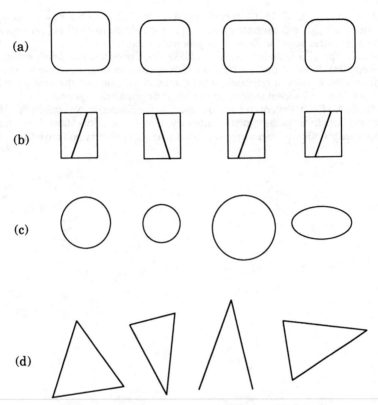

Figure 6.30 Which shape is the odd one out in each row?

drawings with three the same and a fourth as the odd one out. They challenge each other to find the odd one out. Discussion about why the three are the same and the fourth is different will bring out all the fundamental geometric concepts associated with transformation and equivalence that have been the theme of this final chapter.

SUGGESTIONS FOR FURTHER READING

Bright, G.W. and Harvey, J.G. (1988) 'Learning and fun with geometry games', *Arithmetic Teacher*, Vol. 35, no. 8, pp. 22–6. (Bright and Harvey describe some geometry games that require children to visualize geometric properties, analyse them and make informal deductions in an interesting and challenging way.)

Glenn, J.A. (ed.) (1979) *Children Learning Geometry: A Handbook for Teachers*, Harper & Row, London. (This book considers the teaching of geometry in the early years of schooling.)

Larke, P.J. (1988) 'Geometric extravaganza: spicing up geometry', *Arithmetic Teacher*,

Vol. 36, no. 1, pp. 12–16. (A very practical article that describes how to set up a geometry fair that will generate opportunities for children to construct projects and offer meaningful ways for them to use geometric concepts.)

Sicklick, F., Turkel, S.B. and Curcio, F.R. (1988) 'The transformation game', *Arithmetic Teacher*, Vol. 36, no. 2, pp. 37–41. (This article outlines an intriguing game for juniors that uses the notions of reflection, translation and rotation and that is designed to sharpen children's spatial abilities and enrich their geometric experience.)

Woodman, A. (1987) 'Patterns before your eyes', *Junior Education*, November, pp. 24–5. (In this article a primary-maths advisory teacher describes how home-made kaleidoscopes offer an interesting way to learn about symmetry and angles.)

BOOKS FOR FURTHER READING

Burton, L. (1984) *Thinking Things Through: Problem Solving in Mathematics*, Blackwell, Oxford. (This is a useful and thought-provoking book for those interested in mathematical problem-solving in the primary years.)

Buxton, L. (1981) *Do You Panic about Maths?*, Heinemann, London. (The title says it all! A reassuring and readable book for those with little confidence in their mathematical abilities.)

Carpenter, T.P., Moser, J.M. and Romberg, T.A. (eds.) (1982) *Addition and Subtraction: A Cognitive Perspective*, Lawrence Erlbaum Associates, Hillsdale, NJ. (This book comprises a series of interesting readings contributed by a distinguished collection of academics.)

Desforges, C. and Cockburn, A.D. (1987) *Understanding the Mathematics Teacher: A Study of Practice in the First School*, Falmer Press, Lewes. (Based on classroom research, this book gives insight into mathematics education in the early years of schooling and provides teachers with an understanding of the contraints under which they work.)

Dickson, L., Brown, M. and Gibson, O. (1984) *Children Learning Mathematics*, Cassell Education for the Schools Council, London. (This book presents a detailed review of highly-relevant research in the teaching and learning of mathematics.)

Floyd, A. (ed.) (1981) *Developing Mathematical Thinking*, Addison-Wesley in association with the Open University, Wokingham. (An Open University text that contains a wide range of useful readings for those interested in mathematics education.)

Gelman, R. and Gallistel, C.R. (1978) *The Child's Understanding of Number*, Harvard University Press, Cambridge, Mass. (Gelman and Gallistel's work challenges the traditional view of young children's cognitive incapacity. On the basis of extensive research they consider when and how numerical skills are acquired.)

Glenn, J.A. (ed.) (1979) *Children Learning Geometry*, Harper & Row, London. (A mathematically-sound and practical book written for practising or intending teachers in the 5–9 age range.)

Glenn, J.A. (ed.) (1980) *Children Learn to Measure*, Harper & Row, London. (A handbook for teachers that provides a background discussion of measurement and step-by-step suggestions for developing the necessary measurements skills and concepts in 5–11-year-olds.)

Hughes, M. (1986) *Children and Number: Difficulties in Learning Mathematics*, Blackwell, Oxford. (In his book, Hughes considers pre-schoolers' substantial knowledge of number and the difficulties they encounter when presented with the formal, written symbolism of the infant classroom.)

Kamii, C. (1985) *Young Children Reinvent Arithmetic*, Teachers' College Press, New York, NY. (One of the rare books that not only gives details of tried and tested mathematical games but that also considers their importance in fostering mathematical development and understanding.)

Skemp, R.R. (1986) *The Psychology of Learning Mathematics*, Penguin, Harmondsworth. (An up-dated version of Skemp's classic account of mathematics education from a psychologist's and a mathematician's viewpoint.)

Thyer, D. and Maggs, J. (2nd ed. 1981) *Teaching Mathematics to Young Children*, Holt Education, Eastbourne. (This book offers practical guidelines for those teaching, or intending to teach, mathematics to children in the 5–8 age-range.)

INDEX